PRIVATE INTERNATIONAL LAW

OF CORPORATIONS

Maria Kaurakova

Published in November 2017

by

Spiramus Press Ltd
102 Blandford Street
London W1U 8AG
Telephone +44 20 7224 0080

www.spiramus.com

© Spiramus Press Ltd

ISBN Paperback 9781910151679

ISBN Digital   9781910151761

British Library Cataloguing-in-Publication Data.

A catalogue record for this book is available from the British Library.

The right of Maria Kaurakova to be identified as the author of this work has been asserted by him in accordance with the Copyright, Designs and Patents Act, 1988.

Printed and bound in Great Britain by Grosvenor Group, UK.

Contents

Contents...iii

INTRODUCTION 1

1. NATURE AND ESSENCE OF PRIVATE INTERNATIONAL LAW.......3
    1.1.   On legal categories of a rule of law and a conflict of law rule........14
    1.2.   Narrow and broad conceptions of a rule of law 26

2. DISTINGUISHING MARKS OF PRIVATE INTERNATIONAL LAW
OF CORPORATIONS 33
    2.1.   Formal attributes of private international law of corporations 39
    2.2.   Terminological apparatus of private international law of
           corporations...44
    2.3.   On right and wrong principles in private international law of
           corporations...53
      2.3.1.   *Multinational corporations* 55
    2.4.   On questionable points of private international law of corporations
          60

3. SCOPE OF PRIVATE INTERNATIONAL LAW OF CORPORATIONS
    69
    3.1.   Particulars of the use of *lex personalis* 79
    3.2.   Particulars of the use of *lex societatis*...87
    3.3.   Particulars of the use of *lex loci*..95
    3.4.   Particulars of the use of *lex voluntatis*...107
    3.5.   International jurisdiction over cross-border corporate disputes and
           other disputes closely connected with them (cause, particulars and
           effect) 114
      3.5.1.   *When foreign corporations are immune from the jurisdiction of*
              foreign national courts 121
      3.5.2.   *Prior conditions for foreign judgements to be enforced* 121
      3.5.3.   *Recognition of foreign decisions relating to corporate and other rights*
              and obligations arising in this connection...122

4. SCALE OF PRIVATE INTERNATIONAL LAW OF CORPORATIONS
    125
    4.1.   Current state of private international law of corporations............131
    4.2.   Prospects and problems of modern private international law of
           corporations...135

5. CONCLUSION 141

GLOSSARY 145

BIBLIOGRAPHY 149

TABLE OF CASES 155

TABLE OF STATUTES 155

INDEX 157

Preface

This book is what its title implies, an attempt to expound as compendiously and systematically as I can on private international law of corporations as a structurally and logically complete legal institute of private international law dealing with one of the most interesting and complicated private law issues of the time. These are legal and jurisdictional problems arising in cross-border corporate and other relations (investment, labour etc.) closely connected with them.

This survey was undertaken in response to pressing needs of legal theory and practice in study, clarification and expounding on main characteristics, scope and boundary of private international law of corporations, guiding legal principles and a manner of dealing with these interesting and complicated private law issues. Because as it appears, there is no idea attracting more attention than the idea of a corporation dealing freely on foreign markets through the proper use of property and labour.

This book aims to meet these needs. It should be of real service to all those dealing with private international law regulation of corporate and other relations closely connected with them from the theoretical or practical points of view.

INTRODUCTION

This book is about the theory of corporations as subjects of private international law.

Law is the main regulatory instrument of sovereign will of a people in a nation. It has no equal in power and significance.

This book aims to show the true extent and depth of legal and jurisdictional problems that states commonly face now. These are problems dealing with allocation of cross-border corporate relations and other relations closely connected with them in the appropriate system of law and jurisdiction.

This work rests on the idea that in the united but diverse and contradictory world founded upon eternal laws, law should be characterized by the same qualities by virtue of the Latin maxim – *accessio cedit principali*. So, the main end of private international law as a separate field of domestic law should be to support these qualities of the world and law bringing order to it.

The world is built upon different kinds of voluntary and involuntary, permanent and temporary groups and associations characterized by a specific nature, character and attributes. These are states and unions of states as the largest groups; different social, economic, cultural and religious institutions; commercial and non-commercial organizations, unions and even families as the smallest associations of individuals.

They communicate with each other in many different ways, in most cases based on social contracts. This book studies the nature and legal effect of part of these relations into which members of these groups or associations (commercial corporations) enter with the sanction of larger groups (sovereign states).

These are corporate law relations extending far beyond territorial limits of one particular well-organized group with its coercive power (a sovereign state). They are part and parcel of a modern socio-economic life of any community fated to grow and prosper under whichever circumstances.

There has never been a short cut to studying the law of corporations. It is a separate field of domestic law premised on the idea of sanctity of labour and property, which when used in conjunction give rise to specific private law relations offering opportunities to individuals in different socio-economic spheres of any community. However, private international law of corporations is more difficult to study, being mainly premised on a comparative analysis of the distinct theory and practice of settlement of cross-border corporate problems arising in any part of the civilized world closely tied by intensive risk-taking interstate trade and commerce.

In the age of globalization, characterized by uncertainty and changing economic circumstances, the task of resolving private international law disputes becomes even more extensive and complicated, requiring much effort and skill to ensure a state in which everything will be in its appropriate place allotted to it by the very nature of things.

There is no doubt that private international law is necessary. There is no better time than now for a detailed study, when challenges before all those dealing with private international law issues in a corporate sphere are huge but never insurmountable. The main aim of this book is to provide a general overview of the current situation.

It is not a mere compilation of national law rules, and particular jurisdictional and other facts, but a manual for jurists, practitioners of law and academics, who need research covering specific legal and jurisdictional issues in a corporate sphere and suggesting a far-reaching penetration into the issue of the place of private international law of corporations in national systems of law, when viewed through institutional, scientific, practical, strategic and economic dimensions.

These are the issues concerned with allocation of cross-border corporate relations and other relations closely connected with them in the appropriate system of law and jurisdiction resting on the idea of distinct public policy with inherent public interest. The success of this specific legal idea depends on avoiding being drawn into the problems of a particular community.

This obviously cannot be limited solely to practical reasons consisting in resolution of legal and jurisdictional problems arising in a corporate law sphere, which has proved to be firm and inviolable. So this book provides a careful study of institutional, scientific, practical, strategic and economic aspects of private international law of corporations as it was, is and ought to be. This is to show what was done, what we have at present and what needs to be done in this specific area in a manner suggesting a simple and concise reasoning within the confines of scientific, systematic and historical treatment of the issue in study.

I believe that I have omitted nothing that would be of great use to the extensive subject matter of this book, and hope that this labour will not be considered as lost and this book will be of interest and value for all those addressing legal and jurisdictional issues arising in the course of the interstate commercial and non-commercial activity of corporations. I hope the reader will be lenient with any possible errors in the present work dealing with a truly complicated legal sphere.

1. NATURE AND ESSENCE OF PRIVATE INTERNATIONAL LAW

At the very outset, I would like to give a detailed exposition of the nature and essence of private international law of corporations as a legal institute of private international law[1]. The study of its nature will enable us place it in a rules-based system. That is a system of private international law accurately framed to remove obstacles to cross-border trade and commerce through aiming to make both choice of law and jurisdiction simple, concise and certain. It is a key issue for many decades to come because trade is more than markets, services, goods, technologies and money. It is new experience, new rules and values underlying these rules, new customs, traditions and certainly new opportunities to those dealing with it.

The study of the essence or the central and most important part of this legal institute may direct us to the answer as to the role or function of private international law of corporations in this system. Since it goes to the heart of the issue, it cannot be avoided, but first we need a short introduction into private international law as the mother law for many legal institutes advanced currently to ensure free movement of persons and transfer of goods, services and technologies on a cross-border (or cross-jurisdictional) basis.

To begin with, private international law is a separate field of law in national systems of law concerned with steady and harmonious exercising of private law relations across borders of distinct sovereign states bound by unique deeply rooted cultural, religious and other customs and traditions as well as peculiar national ideas of the relevant communities. These are sovereign interests of states underlying national theories of law advanced in distinct legal systems to govern private law relations closely connected with two or more distinct sovereign states.

This book will explore how private international law came to influence the minds of the most talented jurists and practitioners of law and through them all those charged with settlement of legal and jurisdictional problems arising in real and good faith private international law disputes using appropriate tools:
- which in operation agreeable to the very nature and unique spirit of private law relations prevent primacy of one national law and

---

[1] In France the term is *"droit international privé"*, in Italy it is *"diritto internazionale private"*, in Russia – "международное частное право" etc.

jurisdiction over the others in the legal world split into numerous territorial systems of law and jurisdictions;[2]

- precluding arbitrary interference with law and jurisdiction having no connection to the disputed private international law relations being brought to court, thus preventing public interests of the appropriate state from being seriously impaired;
- ensuring unity in what cannot be united by the very nature of things.

Private international law is a great development both by jurists and practitioners of law dealing with complicated issues located in different legal systems through presence of a foreign element in the structure of private law relations established between individuals acting singly or jointly with others (e.g. corporations and other associations). Causing conflicts of laws and jurisdictions, this foreign element is the main legal category of private international law. It is traditionally present in the notion of private international law given in the legal doctrine, its terminology and methodology in order to distinguish this field of law from others.

Private international law is a product of conscious battle of the most talented minds adding considerably to the ever-growing body of the relevant science of law and throwing new light on the subject, thus supporting all those who necessarily come after them. It is specifically formulated in distinct legal systems[3] as a logical consequence of extension of the human potential and

---

[2] Therefore we have English private international law, Italian private international law, French private international law etc.

[3] The National Legal Internet Portal of the Republic of Belarus makes this interesting observation, "...the legal system of any state reflects objective laws of the development of society, as well as its historical, national and cultural peculiarities. The Republic of Belarus, like any other state, has its own legal system which has both common features with the legal systems of other countries and its own special characteristics. The legal system of the Republic of Belarus was essentially influenced by those states, which influenced this country in particular historical periods (Poland - during the 17th-18th centuries and Russia - during the 19th-20th centuries). During the most part of the 20th century, Belarus was a part of the Union of Soviet Socialist Republics (USSR) and this fact surely affected the legal system of today's Belarus (its legal culture, formation of the branches of law, etc.) After the break-up of the USSR, the legal system of the Republic of Belarus segregated from the Socialist Law Family. The structure of the legal system of the Republic of Belarus contains three groups of legal elements ("legal phenomena"). The first group includes legal norms, legal principles and legal institutes (normative aspect). The second group contains a complex of legal institutions (organizational aspect). And the third group is formed with a combination of legal

accordingly adopted by them as a principle basis of written law to answer the question as to which law has to be applied in each specific private law case and in which court this particular case has to be settled in a unified and predictable manner in any part of the world.

That is the case when it may be equally governed by two or more states for a foreign element, which tends to its own national public order. And it should be admitted that this answer may be given only by national law and jurisdiction of the appropriate court with respect to a good number of private law issues based on ideas of sovereignty, territoriality and equality of states with rights and obligations under law of nations.

To retrace the history of private international law as it was initially adopted by distinct legal systems through elaboration and incorporation of specific rules (directly applicable rules, conflict of law rules and rules on international jurisdiction) into the national law matrix would make this book much too long. Therefore in this part I will provide a short sketch of the issue in order to show main ideas underlying this field of law and jurisprudence.

From its origins in the twelfth century AD[4] the significance of private international law was immediately and commonly recognized for the formulation of a number of principles readily suitable to answer complicated legal issues and advance the idea of private law in the common for all nations direction. That is the sanctity of individual and real rights once conferred in a distinct legal order and exercised abroad. Besides much importance has always been attributed to this field of law for the predictable resolution of legal disputes arising in civil and business transactions based on these specific principles. They are distinctly formulated in distinct systems of law but express the common idea and the unique spirit of this regulatory instrument in establishing, acknowledging and protecting private law rights and obligations arising in transactions made abroad, between foreign persons or over foreign property, which are also known in the private international law doctrine and practice under the title of extraterritorial or transnational transactions.

Hence, it means that firm adherence to private international law is universally presumed for the crystallized idea as to which tools to use to

---

views, opinions, and conceptions being unique for Belarusian society and standard of legal development". Text: www.law.by/legal-system/general-information.

[4] In this book "territorial systems of law" means national systems of law, as the main sources of law known to the legal world as ensuring internal order and advanced communication on distinct territories.

settle legal and jurisdictional problems arising in separate spheres of private law when several distinct states come into contact for a foreign element present in the structure of legal relations between the parties. This crystallized idea found its way in the relevant three-fold jurisprudence, comprising the following three substantial elements: public interest, governing law and procedural law and correspondingly affecting the character of private international law regulation.

It does not by itself constitute a form of continuation of the private law jurisprudence in its original sense known to the world for several thousand years. Rather it constitutes a systematic exhibition of specific ideas having different origin, meaning and value. They live in national law doctrines and conceptions to study, interpret and apply law in the way to reconcile conflicting regulatory interests of states based on particular canons of distinct jurisdictions to deal with specific legal relations burdened with a foreign element.

And when speaking of law, that encompasses national or foreign law (law of other sovereign persons) governing marital and parental rights, rights of children, rights of inheritance as well as rights of things, rights of obligations and other operative private law rights arising out of a cross-border activity of individuals in their own quality or jointly with others and making up the subject matter of the relevant field of law. And it should be noted that these are not all rights rather those having a particular value for states. As it will be shown later there is a special mechanism of transformation of facts valuable for states[5] into law. We are speaking of private law rights and obligations, which in their part guard natural freedoms duly observed by sovereign states through limiting the initially unlimited nature of the subjective will and granting a right of self-determination in a socio-economic life of a distinct community.

This legal phenomenon rests on the necessity to look beyond strict limits of national systems of law and jurisdictions to allocate private law relations closely connected with two or more separate public orders in the proper system of law and appropriate jurisdiction.

Hence, it means that the main idea of this regulatory instrument is to make a proper choice between:
(1) material law rules of different sovereign states; and
(2) different jurisdictions when governing these relations.

---

[5] Under these facts in the present context we mean acts of individuals.

For this reason this legal field has always been viewed as struggling for the proper territorial system of law and appropriate jurisdiction.

That is a logical consequence of coexistent national laws and jurisdictions characterized by distinct social, economic, political and finally legal substance in each specific private law case burdened with a foreign element and requiring much skill and knowledge from all those dealing with them.

We are speaking of judges and other persons charged with what is known and termed in the legal theory and practice "settlement of conflicts of laws and jurisdictions" taking the shape of contradictory or concurrent regulatory interests over establishment of particular private rights and obligations. It is important to observe in this connection that the resolution of all these legal and jurisdictions problems is the main end of special ruling advanced by the theory and practice of private international law in a manner to present a high degree of generality in order to govern the endless diversity of extremely complicated cross-border private law controversies in a systematic way.

These are separate types of private international law rules:
(1) directly applicable rules;
(2) conflict of law rules; and
(3) rules on international jurisdiction neatly fixed in national systems of law to ensure their proper functioning with respect to these particular cases.

Starting from their formulation many centuries ago, they have long become an integral part of the legal life of advanced communities thus enriching them with a perfect answer to pressing legal and jurisdictional problems of the time, place and circumstances.

Admitting the complexity of these problems, it is not an easy task in itself to solve them in a manner predictable for the parties. Private law cases may be burdened with a good number of foreign elements closely connected with absolutely different states and jurisdictions. This sometimes makes it impossible for law enforcers to give a certain answer as to which court should hear and determine a private international law case and which law to apply to a specific dispute burdened with peculiar circumstances. Besides further difficulties may be revealed with connection to cases when applicable (governing) law refers to another law for the ruling of private law relations (renvoi). That is one of the most complicated issues of this field of law, which I will cover in greater detail in a later chapter.

Following up this line of reasoning, private international law is not a mere collection of rules in national systems of law. It is a solid, durable and practical system composed of specific legal rules and principles worked out in different languages but in a manner converging public interests of different states at one point. That is the one ensuring their common application to the endless variety of private law cases burdened with irregular blending of foreign elements tending to different national public orders. In this observation we think that we have a very clear understanding of what private international law is. It is designed to ensure both public and private law interests through freeing subjects of law from constraints in their way to foreign states, their markets and social infrastructure offering new knowledge and experience from which they may benefit.

To gain this access as well as their activity abroad smooth and continuous, private international law rules and principles are bound together in separate legal institutes by the unity of the definite subject matter and method[6] making them deal with legal and jurisdictional problems of the time and place for the sustainable development of private law relations on a cross-border basis. In unity these legal institutes constitute a separate field of domestic law[7] addressing the problem of conflicting public law interests of states in the private law sphere. And the main point is that these institutes achieve limited purposes inside heterogeneous systems of law in which they succeed through the relevant choice of governing law to be made in the appropriate forum.

This choice is considered as properly made when:

(1) it is not manifestly incompatible with public policy, public security and public health of a state closely and substantially connected with private international law relations and having a legitimate regulatory interest with respect to these relations;

(2) elements of private law relations or legal facts around these legal relations[8] are viewed and considered separately from each other; and

---

[6] It is well noted that in the process of systematization of law that is the idea of the peculiar subject matter and method of law that distinguishes fields of law into distinct structural elements of national systems of law.

[7] The very same idea with respect to the true nature of private international law is given in *Club Resorts Ltd. v. Van Breda [2012] 1 SCR 572* at para 15 [ABA Tab 16]: *"Private international law is in essence domestic law, and it is designed to resolve conflicts between different jurisdictions, the legal systems or rules of different jurisdictions and decisions of courts of different jurisdictions"*.

[8] These may be 1) persons entering into private law relations with cross-border impact; 2) things over which there is private international law dispute; 3) legal facts around private law relations tending to a foreign public order and alike.

(3) lawmakers indicate to law enforcers which element or fact is the most valuable or important and how to determine its legal seat in the national public order.

And it should be separately noted that when making this choice the judge should consider the unity and integrity of the subject matter of the relevant real and good faith private international law dispute for the further proper establishment, ascertainment, recognition and protection of rights. Without following these steps complementing each other, the choice of law with respect to the substance and facts around real, stable and good faith disputes submitted to two or more distinct systems of law for a foreign element in their structure, is absolutely impractical. But that is not the only issue.

After making these steps in the appropriate forum resulting in the choice of governing law, other issues arise as to:

(1) how this law, if it is foreign, should be treated by judges resolving a private international law dispute - as law or as a fact;

(2) what terminology should be used by judges in court at the settlement of distinct real and good faith private international law disputes; and

(3) are there essential difficulties of terminology within the legal sphere in study?

Starting with the first issue, there is no supreme power above the sovereign authority of states. It rests on the idea that for states to grow and prosper in the long run three main functions (legislative, judiciary and executive) should be properly exercised by competent persons of states within legal boundaries set by them.[9] Because , figuratively speaking, these three sovereign powers are head, heart and hands of the body of the sovereign state. From these observations it is easily understood that no foreign law may ever be assumed and treated as law outside the territory of the state, which made it, save for the sanction from the state applying this law to distinct private law relations.

---

[9] In this connection see the text of Monaco Constitution "...*considérant que les institutions de la Principauté doivent être perfectionnées, aussi bien pour répondre aux nécessités d'une bonne administration du pays que pour satisfaire les besoins nouveaux suscités par l'évolution sociale de sa population... Le pouvoir exécutif relève de la haute autorité du Prince. Le pouvoir législatif est exercé par le Prince et le Conseil National. Le pouvoir judiciaire est exercé par les cours et tribunaux.*" (See Preamble and Art. 3 – 5 of Constitution, 1962

Text:www.legimonaco.mc/305/legismclois.nsf/ViewTNC/ba496527b0d37434c125773f 0038354d!Open Document.

The only source of law, legislative, judiciary and executive powers of states delegated to the relevant competent persons is the people under the head of a sovereign state.[10] That is the main idea advanced in the three-fold jurisprudence (public interest, governing law and procedural law) underlying this particular sphere of ruling. It rests on the assertion of private law rights with cross-border impact based on national material law rules, which judges considering a private international law dispute know (in Latin - *jura novit curia*).

Even if there is a gap in national legislation, judges may easily close it using appropriate material law principles because they know how it works or at least should work. Otherwise, these rights are dealt with by law enforcers based on substantive rules of foreign law. They do not know its content (and actually should not know it) and establish it by inviting experts with profound knowledge of this law and mechanisms of its ruling. Gaps, may be closed only by the use of legal principles pertaining to a foreign system of law in a manner as it is done therein, certainly, if this will not put at risk the public policy, public security and public health of the relevant sovereign state[11]. And when we speak of foreign legal principles we also mean foreign

---

[10] For the evidence please turn to fundamental principles of Constitution of the Republic of Malawi, 1994 given in art. 12 of this act ("CRM 1994") *"All legal and political authority of the State derives from the people of Malawi and shall be exercised in accordance with this Constitution solely to serve and protect their interests."*

[11] Thus, for example, all gaps in the Russian legislation should be closed by judges based on chief principles clearly set by Russian lawmaking authorities in Art. 1 of the Civil Code of the Russian Federation (Part One No. 51-FZ of November 30, 1994) ("CC 1994"). These are the ones resting on the sanctity of individual and property rights necessary in the civil law sphere: equality of participants, inadmissibility to arbitrary interference into private affairs, necessity to exercise freely civil rights, guarantee of the reinstatement of civil rights, their protection in the court, inviolability of property and contractual freedom. And it should be noted separately that under civil rights in the present context are meant all and any rights arising from contractual and extra contractual relations as well as other property and personal non-property relations based on (1) equality, (2) autonomy of will and (3) property independence of the participants. Hence, it means that this term embraces all commercial and non-commercial rights, which may ever arise in the private law sphere.

jurisprudence, which is thus employed to determine a private law case placed in the hands of foreign judges.[12]

The main difficulty here arises from intrinsic verbal ambiguities resulting in different names ascribed to the same things in distinct sovereign states, which should be treated in the same way as in foreign jurisdictions.[13] And what is particularly important here is that this difficulty may never be encountered by sovereign states, so the notions of reasonability and justice come in absolutely distinct shapes and forms around the world.

The reality is that these names vary depending on the place, time and circumstances for unique deeply-rooted cultural, religious and other customs and traditions as well as peculiar national ideas being behind these objects and concepts and affecting their names. They all differ in their spirit and this is consistent with the idea of the world split into distinct parts. In this light no one may give a single or a definite name to a thing of the material world to be commonly or consistently used in all states and on all languages. And even if states agree on uniform application of a number of terms to serve a group of states in one particular sphere of socio-economic ruling, this neither means that they will be commonly treated by these states nor that these states stop advancing their own systems of law in the way they find it acceptable.[14]

Other issues I would like to address in the present context include:

- How do states recognize decisions made by foreign courts based on their legislation, which are sacred and inviolable?[15]

---

[12] These are persons facing numerous uncommon legal traditions to which much faith and credit should always be given when considering private law cases closely connected with two or more sovereign states.

[13] For a more objective view please turn to national legislation. Thus, under French law property is immovable, either by its nature (lands and buildings, windmills or watermills, fixed on pillars and forming part of a building) or by its destination (animals and things that the owner of a tenement placed thereon for the use and working of the tenement) or by the object (pipes used to bring water into a house) to which it applies (See Art. 517-524 of French Civil Code. Last amendment translated: Act No. 2013-404 of 17 May 2013 ("FCC 2013").

[14] To support this thesis, read the judgment of the Supreme Court made in *Kennedy v Charity Commissioners*, in which it is kept that "*the development of the common law did not come to an end on the passing of the Human Rights Act 1998. It is in vigorous health and flourishing in many parts of the world which share a common legal tradition*" ([2014] UKSC 20, [2015] AC 455 para 46).

[15] With respect to inviolability of law see the act of the supreme and ultimate source of authority in the republic of Malawi, in which it is given that "*all institutions and*

- What principles or maxims underlie the very idea of reciprocal delimitation of powers when ruling private international law relations?
- What principles or maxims underlie actions of judges or other persons charged with settlement of conflict of law problems in advancing this peculiar type of ruling?
- May these principles or maxims be later viewed as inconsistent with a national idea of private international law of *lex fori*?

Who sets a boundary between proper and improper law and jurisdiction?

To reply these questions means to uncover the true nature of intercourse between nations. Throughout the history of private international law we know that nations agree on this intercourse based initially on the common or general practice with international comity, mutual necessity, common interest, friendship, good neighbourliness, cooperation of states or any other idea underlying it. At the heart of this practice is the sanctity of property and labour rights and interests as well as distinct procedural rights causing states to cooperate when exercised on a cross-border basis.

These distinct ideas lay the foundation for:
(1) particular commands to judges as to which law (and in which forum) will govern private law relations burdened with a foreign element;
(2) the sanctioning of the area of free choice of law and forum to private international law relations arising between the parties;
(3) the authority of national courts over private international law disputes.

That is the principal method of handling conflicting regulatory interests of states in the private law sphere when addressing the issues of the choice of applicable law, international jurisdiction, recognition and enforcement of foreign made decisions.

At present it can hardly be doubted that for the advancement of interstate trade and commerce states should not only refer to foreign law and jurisdiction when establishing, ascertaining, recognizing and protecting distinct legal rights but they should also recognize and enforce decisions made by foreign courts to effect the above-mentioned choice based on the relevant formal mechanism. It rests on international agreements incorporated into a national law matrix and giving rise to the relevant rights and obligations of states with respect to the governance of private law relations. However, states become legally obliged to recognize them then and only then when:

---

persons shall observe and uphold the Constitution and the rule of law and no institution or person shall stand above the law" (Art. 12 of CRM 1994).

(1) a breach of their public interests is precluded either before or on the date of their enforcement; and

(2) these decisions are made by foreign courts commensurate with commands given by lex fori setting the boundary between proper and improper law and jurisdiction.

Here I would like to point out that details of each peculiar case should never be tried based on subjective reasoning which is founded on rational or irrational judgments. This means that the interests of immediate parties of private international law relations may not exercise influence over effect of conflict of law regulation in the appropriate forum except for the area of the free choice of law and jurisdiction to the exclusion of any others when it accords with the sovereign (supreme) will of the relevant state. Besides a judge should not be any even slightest interested in the settlement of an issue in a way incompatible with what is given by conflict of law rules.

The particular value of private international law is to be expected in a period with harmonized national legal acts and uniform international rulings. In the best tradition of this field of law respecting interests of all states with rights and obligations under the law of nations even those which voice is barely audible on economic and political arenas of the time, common concession is given to laws produced by different sovereign states constructing their own systems of law.

For this very reason in this book reference is made to legal acts of all legal systems. Its particular value and importance in the sphere of regulation of private law relations is maintained by a specific idea of law, which by itself is initially a purely national development manifesting a specific spirit of a particular community extending its sovereignty over a separate territory in a general or public manner.[16]

Attaching particular importance to the nature of law, we cannot ignore the fact that law as a sovereign idea of the absolute or supreme power of a state

---

[16] The same idea in relation to the common law was expressed by a well-known English judge, Lord Neuberger of Abbotsbury at his speech in the Faculty of Law of the National University of Singapore in August 2016 *"...the common law in England is now developing of its own accord as it should and as it always has done, as part of, and within the confines of, our unique constitutional system. And it doing so it will incorporate human rights bearing in mind the contents of the Convention, but equally importantly also bearing in mind that the development of the common law should not be limited or controlled by the scope of the Convention, decision of the Strasbourg court"* (see "Has the identity of the English Common Law been eroded by EU Laws and the European Convention On Human Rights?").

ensuring internal order and advanced communication on a definite territory is universally accepted. Law forms an integral part of the fabric of the relevant community. It has always been placed on a peculiar logic, specific experience and distinct reasoning and thus represents itself nothing else than delimitation of interests (public or private) or wills (subjective and objective) over a number of issues.

This idea has different manifestations in definite rules of law passed by national legislators to comport with specific societal conditions of communities in specific territories. That is the first fundamental issue (territorial operation of law and private international law as a separate field of law), which I would like to discuss. The next is the mutual relationship or connection between rules of law and conflict of law rules, which this specific field of law (private international law) employs when resolving complicated legal problems arising in the corporate and other spheres closely connected with this.

1.1. On legal categories of a rule of law and a conflict of law rule

To begin with it should be noted that both natural and human laws extending their power and control over all types of human activity are the most powerful instruments employed to ensure order in all parts of the world. A close look at specific rules bringing order into private law relations with cross-border impact is required. This study will start two legal categories. These are "rule of law" as a form of expression of human law in general and "conflict of law rule" as a form of expression of a separate field of human law, which is private international law.

To show a mutual relationship or connection between them based on a survey of their core features means to throw some light on the nature, character, essence and effect of law, which is national law, and private international law as a separate field of national law. Because law is an abstract term, it has distinct meaning in different states, including that of a natural justice as a general idea and a specific technique as to how to realise this idea. They are brought together to guide the conduct of the contracted parties in a particular sphere of socio-economic relations in a manner predictable both for public and private law subjects and thus meet their distinct interests. And what is particularly important is that this meaning of law may never be harmonized. Likewise, we may never have one language (e.g. English, French or Italian) rather numerous different languages (e.g. Russian, Italian, French, German) in this united but diverse and contradictory world, which rests on fixed laws requiring free access of all people to any part of the world based on common rights and obligations to be ensured by states through appropriate functionaries.[17]

The point is that only rules of law may give us a clear and concise understanding of what law, this truly powerful instrument of the supreme authority of states, is. Because law forming an integral part of the community's fabric lives and undergoes changes in these distinct forms exemplifying asynchronous and differential development of law or sometimes even regress of law. But currently there is absolutely no system of law, the development of which has come to an end or no longer responds to socio-economic trends and concerns. Without this knowledge we would hardly succeed in complete evaluation of the main end of this legal institute (private international law of corporations) and a field of law (private international law) in general. Moreover, it is absolutely essential to appreciate the significance and role of this field of law in systems of private law of distinct sovereign states.

Whenever we speak of law it is important to start with than the theory of law, where there is ample material addressing all these issues. It is aimed at assigning peculiar functions to law as a system composed by consistent elements each playing a particular role through guiding regular and irregular events in a socio-economic life of any community in a predictable manner. They all pursue their own ends in conformity with specific interests of a community, which life this law serves.

Without due regard to a present-day theory of law there can be no serious analysis of legal problems arising in a socio-economic life of a definite community and therefore there may not be any chance to elaborate proper means to settle them. Because we all know that nothing ever comes from nothing, or in other words, everything in this material world governed by a good number of social rules (customs, mores, folkways, legal rules and principles etc.) has its cause and effect.[18] Therefore, accomplishment of this end is guided by the interests of a community resting on the close study of

---

[17] To enter new markets individuals need to have rights to come and make private law deals duly recognized by host states through the relevant competent persons.

[18] In law the main source of all knowledge necessary for drafting rules appropriated for the socio-economic reality of the distinct community is jurisprudence. Looking at national legal acts, for example, in Syria, the main source of legislation is Islamic jurisprudence. This is given in Art. 4 of the Constitution adopted on 13 March 1973 ("C 1973"). For the detailed exposition of the scope of Islamic or Muslim jurisprudence See Duncan B. Macdonald. 1903. *"Development of Muslim Theology, Jurisprudence and Constitutional Theory,"* Charles Scribner's Sons, New York.

conditions of its life, which should always be met for the further continuing perfection of law to respond to new socio-economic circumstances.

In this theory of law resting on specific ideas of the subject matter and method of law, rules of law are a basic material on which rests the study of law as well as problems, which law faces when governing the endless variety of socio-economic relations. And when we speak of them in detail, it has to be observed that though many other conceptions may be developed in the national law doctrine or court practice, we insist on the one resting on the very idea that the nature of legal rules is unchangeable. In line with other types of social rules, they are a product of the sovereign will and power of the people inhabiting a distinct territory and therefore reflect with different intensity cultural and other deeply rooted customs and traditions of the particular place as well as its unique spirit taken at the definite time and circumstances.

Here we come to the mechanism of ruling. Being an objective side of law, rules of law transform numerous socio-economic relations into which individuals enter pursuing different goals from the category of fact, presenting itself in their actual activity, to a category of law. We are speaking of legal relations or relations having support and protection in law and forming a category of the subjective side of law.

When considered in unity these are two sides of law. One rests on the objective (popular) will or will of sovereign persons and has no intrinsic value without being of practical use for the human activity (capacity of being operative). The other is grounded upon the subjective will of the parties of private law relations, which should always be limited to their interests as well as interests of a home state in general. These two sides of law supplement each other and show delimitation of popular and unpopular interests in the ruling of the heterogeneous human activity held inside a separate community.[19]

---

[19] By way of illustration, look at the following rule: *"No company, association, or partnership consisting of more than ten persons shall be formed for the purpose of carrying on the business of banking, unless it is registered as a company under this Act, or is formed in pursuance of some other Act or law or Letters Patent"* (see Part 1 of Companies Act of Belize, 2003). One may find two wills complementing each other in this short rule. That is the one inherent to a sovereign state resting on the idea to ensure and protect third parties interests in the banking sphere in case of large partnerships, and the one of individuals pursuing the end to carry out this activity jointly, in some common financial interest. The very same idea is given in Art 515 of Companies Act of Botswana, 2007 *"No company, association, syndicate or partnership consisting of more than 20 persons shall be formed in Botswana for the purpose of carrying*

With regard to a legal activity given above, it should be noted that states ensure its proper development by formulating categories of legal rights and obligations, which as it is kept in distinct instruments of the governing national law, are duly established, acknowledged and protected through annexation of rights of action to operative legal rights. It is evident that through the intrinsic power of sovereign states rooted in the very nature of these regulatory tools, the main function of rules of law consists in raising consciousness and responsibility on issues sensitive for each person and a community as a whole.

Based on this, they guide not all relations but only those which have a particular importance for a community, the main attributes of which are companionship and interdependence of unique ideas, customs and traditions. However, there are also other, special functions of rules of law, which make their particular role in the governance of a social life of any community absolutely unchallenged. Rules of law preclude breaches of private and public law rights and interests or exclude their adverse effect and thus ensure peaceful and harmonious development of a community.

With respect to this there is another consideration of great importance. That is the classification of rules of law governing the endless variety of socio-economic relations. It is evident that rules of law are a product of the time and place with different historical and ideological foundation. It is also evident that under the title of rules of law there are different ordinances distinctly affecting the life of the relevant communities. This results in systematization of law in a way peculiar for the relevant community.

This book aims to rise above particulars of the place and try to show the true extent and depth of problems concerned with allocation of cross-border corporate relations and other relations closely connected with them that states commonly face now in the appropriate system of law and jurisdiction. So, here I would like to give a classification of the rules of law meeting this end. That is the one resting, in particular, on:

-   **sphere of application (e.g. private or public law sphere).** We may distinguish private and public law rules giving rise to rights, legal interests, privileges, power and immunities as distinct legal forms of freedom as well as duties and liability as forms of legal ties binding subjects of law to particular actions or refraining them from making these actions;

---

on any business that has for its object the acquisition of gain by the company, association, syndicate or partnership, or by the individual members thereof, unless it is registered as a company under this Act or is formed in pursuance of some other law".

- **nature of ruling.** All rules of law fall into several main categories and thus bear the name of ethical, technical, procedural and other rules. Their number is enormous as enormous is the number of cases to which these rules apply. All these rules pursue different ends, to which much value is assigned in relevant communities. As a rule they are kept apart from each other in divergent forms of law and have distinct effect in different spheres of a socio-economic life of these communities. Nevertheless, they are always viewed in unity supplementing each other, because they do not have a separate value by themselves;
- **character of ruling.** All rules of law fall into two main categories: mandatory and default (or otherwise optional) rules. This character exerts material effect on legal consequences of failure to keep or observe them. Thus, infringement of mandatory rules triggers sanctions as a logically inevitable consequence of voluntary actions to this effect;
- **essence of ruling.** Affecting its form all rules fall into the following types: rules-principles, rules-definitions, rules-statements etc.
- **end of ruling** (e.g. to resolve a material law dispute or private international law dispute). We may distinguish material law rules, conflict of law rules and international jurisdiction rules;
- **main idea of ruling in the private international law sphere.** We may distinguish directly applicable rules to the exclusion of all and any legal problems arising in the private law sphere based on the idea of public interest advanced in numerous legal systems, and conflict of law rules premised on the idea of private interests to be protected at the settlement of conflict of law problems etc.

At the end of this non-exclusive classification of rules of law I have mentioned conflict of law rules as main legal tools to deal with problems of conflicting regulatory interests of two or more sovereign states in the private law sphere. And in clarifying what conflict of law rules are, it appears reasonable to state what they definitely are not.

It may be said that, in the first place, they do not fall under the category of material law rules. Conflict of law rules are conditioned by the aim to resolve legal problems arising between states rather than persons. They lack moral import and do not directly protect the private law rights and interests most sensitive for private and sovereign persons. At the same time, conflict of law rules unblock remaining barriers to trade and commerce without which no sovereign state may flourish.

These are concurrent interests of two or more states in the ruling of legal relations, being a voluntary or involuntary exchange of legal rights and obligations in the private law sphere and characterized by formal equality of those entering into them.[20] Therefore, material law rules as a general term embracing different types of rules deal with categories of private law rights and obligations, which are accordingly defined in applicable legal instruments, whereas conflict of law rules are mainly and exclusively concerned with categories of private international law rights and obligations.

The relation between legal categories of rights and obligations in material and conflict of law spheres should be regarded as the same legal phenomena characterizing subjects of a private law activity with intrinsic full legal capacity conceded by home states and recognized by host states. There is only one distinction. They are viewed through different legal prisms.

Thus, for example, in case of disputes arising out of cross-border commercial and non-commercial relations judges and other persons charged with their consideration use categories pertaining to a conflict of law sphere. The choice of governing law categories of material law comes into use only upon completion of this process.

As a result, establishment, acknowledgment and protection of legal rights and obligations are dealt with based on applicable substantive law rules. From this we may conclude that there is a relative relation between legal categories of rights and obligations in material and conflict of law spheres. These are legal phenomena, which commencement or termination rely on a number of closely connected legal facts (e.g. expiration of time, supply of defective goods).

Surveying both types of legal rules in different systems, it immediately becomes apparent where essential points of difference between two of them arise. It is sufficiently recognized that rules of law are primary legal tools in national systems of law offering consistency when employing their own sources of written law ensuring united and uniform (or predictable) regulation in any part of the relevant community.

---

[20] These are physical and legal persons, in some cases even states acting as purchasers or sellers or in another similar non-sovereign capacity. In that instance states fall from their *"high estate of the supreme power and authority"* and deal in the same quality as other subjects of private law. For the evidence see Art. 1 and 2 of CC 1994, in which it is given that *"the civil legislation shall be based on recognizing the equality of participants in the relationships regulated by it..."* and *"...both the citizens and the legal entities may be the participants of the relations, regulated by the civil legislation. The Russian Federation, the subjects of the Russian Federation and the municipal entities may also participate in the relations, regulated by the civil legislation* (Art. 124).

The structure of legal rules varies along numerous lines in response to some particular end they pursue in different spheres of the socio-economic life of the relevant communities. The classical logical structure of material rules of law appears to encompass hypothesis, disposition and sanction.[21] Nevertheless, in conflict of law rules, there are no duties and as a consequence no sanctions preventing persons from violations.

The structure of a conflict of law rule consists of:

(1) hypothesis (showing which cases come within the purview of this rule); and

(2) disposition (making reference to law applicable to private law relations considered in the high degree of generality for the regulation of typical for a particular jurisdiction relations, thus leaving aside specific conditions of each particular case, which may never be the same).[22]

It is understood that conflict of law rules provide for hypothetic judgments or better commands addressed to law enforcers as to what law has to be applied to regular private law relations burdened with a number of legal facts tending to different public orders with which these legal facts are closely connected. Each private law relation or act forms a part of the relevant public order. In other words, a definite public interest lies behind the conduct of individuals acting singly or jointly (e.g. corporations, states). That is the home or host public order sanctioning this private law relation or act and determining whether it was effected to ensure private law rights and obligations arising in this respect. And they do not immediately connect any legal consequences with observance or non-observance of these judgments or command, unlike in material law rules.

---

[21] An example in French law, provides that *"guardianship is a personal office. It does not extend to a guardian's spouse. Where, however, that spouse intrudes into the management of the ward's patrimony, he or she becomes jointly and severally liable with the guardian for all management subsequent to the intrusion"* (see Art. 418 of FCC 2013.

[22] Thus, for example, under Spanish law *"possession, ownership and other rights over immovable property and publicity thereof shall be governed by the law of the place where such property is located"* (see Art. 10 of Spanish Civil Code, 2009 ("SCC 2009"). Between hypothesis (*possession, ownership and other rights over immovable property and publicity thereof*) and disposition (*law of the place where such property is located*) in the two-tier structure of conflict of law rules may be imperative (e.g. shall/should/ought to be governed by law of this or that country) or descriptive connection (e.g. is governed by the law of this or that country) depending on the character of the particular conflict of law rule (mandatory, default or alternative). In disposition of this rule may be reference to one particular state (rules applying a single connecting factor) or different states having regulatory interests over private law relations (rules with differentiated connection).

This all affects the functioning of conflict of law rules. It seems to be evident that when dealing with conflicting regulatory interests of states in the private law sphere it should rest on interests of fraternity and reciprocity.[23] Going deeper into this issue, it becomes apparent that that is the manner of dealing with numerous complicated private law issues; too many to be discussed or even enumerated. Conflict of law rules address them suggesting a multi-stage process starting from the study of private international law relations for the further choice of law closely and/or substantially connected with them, and ensuring private law rights and interests of those who entered into them, based on material law rules of the governing law.

A significant number of issues with which conflict of law rules are concerned, are found in different legal systems depending on the particulars of private law cases brought to court.[24] And these issues may be solved only in this multi-stage approach. So far the main function of conflict of law rules consists in development of good practice in resolving private international law disputes in a cross-border activity both in the interests of those entering into them and those to which these persons are subjected to by the very idea of the state sovereignty extending its force over a definite territory. And there is a reason for that. All states are interdependent, both in public and private international law spheres.

For this reason the role of law enforcers consists in that they act within the confines of conflict of law rules ensuring submission to proper law[25] of specific private law relations with foreign elements, being of independent jural significance and having a ripple effect on all other elements. Being practical, this submission derives from the very idea that all private law relations are seated in definite public orders and only competent public orders may decide over the fate of private law rights and obligations. It is evident therefore that private international law is the ordaining law, which

---

[23] In this connection it is worth citing Emperor Caesar Flavius Justinian words given in the book of Institutes "...*the imperial majesty should be armed with laws as well as glorified with arms, that there may be good government in times both of war and of peace, and the ruler of Rome may not only be victorious over his enemies, but may show himself as scrupulously regardful of justice as triumphant over his conquered foes..*".

[24] For this reason persons entering into cross-border legal relations should apply a cost-effective approach in the anticipating stage with the object of precluding losses arising in private international law disputes submitted to foreign law and jurisdiction.

[25] Under the term "proper law" we mean a system of material law rules closely connected with these relations (be it national or foreign law).

authorizes resolution of conflict of law problems and settles them in a way acceptable to sovereign states putting it forward.

Conflict of law rules hold which law has to be applied in cases with a number of general circumstances attributable to private international law cases, when material law rules are inadequate to decide what should or should not be done, because they mainly rest on the moral rather than rational foundation. And through the choice of the governing law they guide the parties of private international law relations with certainty concerning a general effect of their relations, which sometimes may not be on the surface because of their complexity.

This capacity is sanctioned by a specific substance of conflict of law rules. The mechanism by which conflict of law rules function rests on the very idea of the common practice set by sovereign states as to the manner to reconcile conflicting interests in a private law sphere. This idea presupposes the co-existence of different material law rules comporting to specific place, time and circumstances and exercising much influence on a socio-economic life of communities.

We need to look at the common practice for the following reasons. First, we have to acknowledge that, as it has already been said, in the private international law sphere all states act independently, by their sovereign will and based on their own legislation. Second, with the aim of creating and protecting certain private international law rights presuming their origin from the legislative power of other states, these states have to assume and extend the idea of legitimacy of these rights and therefore recognize them on just and equitable principles.[26] Third, these principles underlie actions of states as if they are set by international agreements having obligatory force for them when there may not be any, rather their common interest, to ensure predictable execution of private law relations on a cross-border basis.

This activity resting on the common practice of dealing with conflicting interests of states in a private law sphere and ensuring reciprocity[27] in

---

[26] With a view to the particular nature, character and value of these rights in separate sovereign states their protection is ensured by Constitutions. See Art. 5 of Brazil's Constitution, 1988 with amendments through 2014 ("BC 1988")"*everyone is equal before the law, with no distinction whatsoever, guaranteeing to Brazilians and foreigners residing in the Country the inviolability of the rights to life, liberty, equality, security and property...*".

[27] Thus, for example, reciprocity is necessary in such issues sensitive for national public orders as matters of procedure, which are traditionally submitted to the law of the forum save for particular cases when courts may apply the limitation rules of the *lex causae* in which "*a court in England and Wales, in exercising in pursuance of*

addressing complicated private international law issues keeps necessary harmony and order in the legal sphere within definite terms accepted by them.

With respect to "informal" duties of sovereign states in the sphere of governance of private law relations closely connected with two or more distinct public orders, their non-fulfilment will not trigger international law sanctions. This will rather entail the same approach (retortions) from other states, whose interests were accordingly affected. The reason is evident - these duties are imperative by themselves. They rest on the very idea of sovereignty of states and their equality under the law of nations and therefore do not need any support in distinct legal instruments to this effect.

For this reason, private international law may be characterized as a field of national law which in most cases reflects sublimity and intrinsic dignity of national law maxims resting on objective things (reality) correspondingly affecting the conscience of those making law in favour of just settlement of private international law disputes rather than mere subjective impulses affording solution based on selfish reasons negatively affecting rights and interests of those who called for a state as a person to judge over terms and effect of these rights exercising.

The ultimate test of any social rules is their stability, efficiency and utility. This brings us to the question as to whether conflict of law rules maintain the same order and harmony in life of communities as other legal rules entering in their turn into the term "social rules". These are order and harmony as two things allowing communities to grow and prosper. In order to answer this question we need to show the correlation between conflict of law rules and material law rules as two separate but closely connected types of rules.

Though there is no fundamental difference between them, still they are different. And this difference lies in their approaches. Conflict of law rules furnish solutions of issues relevant to applicable law and jurisdiction resting upon *utility*, while material law rules resolve private law disputes of the parties based on something more important than utility (which may never be the only criterion), and that is *justice*.

Between these two categories (utility as a practical category and justice as a philosophical category), there is no place for the opposition, but they are

---

subsection (1) (a) above any discretion conferred by the law of any other country, shall so far as practicable exercise that discretion in the manner in which it is exercised in comparable cases by the courts of that other country". (Section 1, subsection 4 of the Foreign Limitation Periods Act 1984).

evidently different. This gives us enough reasons to distinguish conflict of law rules, being premised on utility for states, from material law rules resting on justice. The correlation between these two types of rules of law may be shown in this way: a corporate law rule guides internal and external relations of corporations in a just manner; a conflict of law rule refers to a system of material law rules in a predictable and useful manner appearing in their common guidance notwithstanding a cross-border nature of these relations. But wherever something unjust is found in the construction of a conflict of law rule, it should not be applied. Because it is contrary to the very substance of law resting on higher (natural) laws.

However, conflict of law rules should not be considered separately from material law rules. Conflict of law rules are shaped independently from material law rules, but they are not complete and sufficient in themselves. For this reason their operation precedes, rather precludes, the application of material law rules. It is sufficiently recognized that material law rules are premised on certain principles guiding human actions, while conflict of law rulesare based on a specific mechanism of choice of law closely and/or substantially connected with private law relations in dispute. Thus they may never be considered apart from each other. Both of them tend to keep national law in the most perfect form and both form an integral part of legal rules employed by states for the governance of different types of the socio-economic activity carried out in separate communities. This means that conflict of law rules are characterized by all the qualities of legislatively efficient rules (stability, efficiency and utility).

Conflict of law rules are not international law rules established by unions of sovereign states to govern public law relations arising between them based on international law principles, customs and traditions. They have nothing in common with international law rules. Nevertheless, the word "international" is present in their title to indicate a specific nature of private law relations, to which these legal rules apply.

For the elements in the structure of private law relations "seated" in distinct legal orders, these relations are closely connected with more than one state and one law. This entails conflicting regulatory interests of separate sovereign states over these relations and thus makes "founding fathers of private international law" find an element of internationality in these private law relations for their further allocation in the proper system of law. That is the element serving as evidence of communication or dealings between distinct communities in their peculiar sovereign way.

But taking into account a purely national nature of law and correspondingly private law relations, private international law relations are subjected to domestic conflict and material law rules peculiar to a particular people vested with sovereignty to be exercised within distinct territorial bounds.[28]

In the third place, because of a specific intermediary role of conflict of law rules in private law regulation they do not take immediate effect on the parties of legal relations. They set bounds to external liberty of law enforcers when resolving problems concerned with conflicting regulatory interests of distinct sovereign states called for the accurate observance of strict written law. Thus, it should be clear that law enforcers act in the manner as it is determined by these rules, because that is their obligation to be fulfilled in accordance with letter of law.[29] And only after making this choice of law, certain effect may be given to definite private law rights and obligations of the parties dealing on a cross-border basis.

As it may be seen from the above, conflict of law rules are a real phenomenon of a juridical life resting on a definite positive practice blazing the path through a forest of legal problems. Among main characteristics of conflict of law rules are abstractedness, neutrality, relative uniformity, formal stability, indispensable and intermediary character of specific legal requirements, employed by sovereign states, and particular practical utility. They rest on the very idea of the necessity to find a legal seat of private law relations with a foreign element in a proper system of law using appropriate legal tools to solve this peculiar legal issue.[30]

Therefore, they are not destined to be confined to narrow limits of one enacting state and its law. They rather set definite limits within which law enforcers should keep their actions in the choice of applicable or governing law. But this choice may be made in favour of any state and any law for further material law regulation, if this does not infringe public interests underlying peculiar legal rules employed in a private international law

---

[28] See Art. 2 and Art. 12 of C 1973 *"sovereignty is vested in the people, who exercise it in accordance with this Constitution"*. Of particularl importance is that *"the state is at the people's service. Its establishments seeks to protect the fundamental rights of the citizens and develop their lives. It also seeks to support the political organizations in order to bring about self-development"*.

[29] Think of the case when a foreign judge justifies non-application of foreign law based on defects which may be found in it. This judge may not be above a foreign legislator to search and discover defects in law passed by a separate sovereign state. Legislative power is one of three main powers exercised solely by states through authorized persons, and that is the idea of sovereignty underlying their functioning, which may never be ignored.

[30] That is a peculiar manner of acting in development of a particular idea.

sphere. These are directly applicable rules, conflict of law rules or international jurisdiction rules.

Based on these characteristics, specific "conflict of law rules" can be delineated commonly used both in the legal theory and practice to rules furnishing solutions to peculiar legal problems according to their object. For that reason to be called a conflict of law rule a rule should be characterized by the unity of the aim and means specifically devised for the settlement of legal problems arising in private law relations closely connected with two or more different national public orders resulting from coexistence of different national laws and jurisdictions and coming this way into contact. It suggests relations between different states, though in fact they may not exist at all.

Consequently, conflict of law rules are rules for delimitation of legitimate regulatory interests of different states in private law relations closely connected with more than one state. Notwithstanding this delimitation of interests in law making and law enforcement techniques which denote very clearly their distinct ideas on this issue, these interests always converge at one point - to ensure predictable settlement of conflict of law problems in private law cases burdened with foreign elements. And this settlement is undertaken in a manner having no analogies in its nature but ensuring common satisfaction.

The above observations enable us to conclude that "rules of law" is a generic term embracing different legal tools (e.g. conflict of law rules, material law rules) correlating with the main idea to ensure peace and harmony in a distinct community as a well-organized permanent group by means of state control of the human activity. To meet this end in the private international law sphere conflict of law rules address the issue of a fundamental relation between one well-organized group and another over the right to hear and rule distinct private law cases, while material law rules directly deal with them by establishing, recognizing and protecting private law rights and obligations.

1.2. Narrow and broad conceptions of a rule of law

For sovereign will (traditionally kept as an objective one) to become binding towards unlimited number of subordinate persons (nationals or residents) it has been packaged in the form of rules of law, which vary depending on the place, time and circumstances exercising much influence on them. Earlier in the book I have already addressed the issue of what is the correlation between a rule of law, a legal tool to remedy the evil in a socio-economic life of the relevant community, and a conflict of law rule devised to reconcile conflicting interests of states in a private law sphere in a logical and consistent with public interests way. But I need to throw some light on what it is, based on narrow and broad conceptions of a rule of law carefully formulated by theories advancing different approaches to the original conditions of the formation of law.

Over the centuries different scope was ascribed to a legal and normative notion "rule of law", which in line with other human law notions is susceptible to numerous external influences. This mainly reflects the general tendency of legal development welcomed in most advanced jurisdictions. Sometimes it goes unnoticed when considered through the prism of revolutionary changes. However, facts mainly contradict this. There has always been much discussion upon the question, what a rule of law is. And now I would like to highlight two main conceptions of rules of law, which are worth mentioning and try to emphasize their aim and content using legal and philosophical approaches when appropriate.

To begin with, there is a narrow conception of a rule of law, which I would like to address in detail so as to explain a legal notion of a rule of law without enlarging the scope of this subject. This conception finds its root in the theory of state sovereignty, upon which common rights to law making, law enforcing and judging characterize each state. There is nobody above the state to exercise these rights, which ensures inalienable equality of states as the only supreme power running the world.

In this first narrow sense, rules of law are a separate type of social rule. They rest on the order of sovereign states, guide all forms of the human activity in different spheres of the socio-economic life of communities and form their integral part. In accordance with this theory, advancing the idea of supremacy of law, social rules should meet the following requirements, which we hold as essential ones. They should be:

(1) set by persons specifically authorized by states (legislators and/or judges, other persons in accordance with a legal tradition);

(2) expressed in a concise, intelligible and non-discriminatory manner to govern different types of the human activity and therefore protect certain interests essential for sovereign states; and

(3) accompanied by sanctions to be inflicted on those who breach these ordinances to induce people to follow them.

These are only the main criteria, which may lay a line of separation between rules of law, this manifestation of peculiar power, and other social and moral rules, customs and regulations recognized by a definite community and being of certain practical use in its actual life in accordance with its unique spirit. However, it is equally interesting and important to observe that rules of law have a social and moral content expressing prevailing sentiments inside a community. They also vary depending on time, place and circumstances. For this reason, rules of law always differ. But this is not the only task we have. As rules of law are divided into two main groups (material law rules and conflict of law rules) we need to know whether conflict of law rules comply with these criteria.

Practice shows that conflict of law rules, though a separate type of legal rules, are not exceptional, save for their lack of sanctions. These are specific ordinances made by the legislative power and expressed in simple and concise formulae to guide the conduct of law enforcers in strict accordance with some objective will when resolving private international law disputes in a predictable way for states under a risk of retortions. For a specific nature and end of ruling, which may not have any separate practical value, they are not equally ranked with material law rules. Nevertheless, we may conclude that they meet the narrow definition of "rules of law".

This definition leaves out all and any prescriptions, orders and regulations made by incompetent persons to the effect to guide the human action in different spheres of the socio-economic life of a separate community. From the study of legal theory we know that no one may give effect to rules of law without due authorization from states under strictly set procedures. This is due to the compulsory nature of legal rules resting on the idea of intrinsic powers of those making them and attaching much importance to lawmaking functions of sovereign persons.[31]

We are also well aware of general requirements of social rules to become mandatory for all those obliged to observe them (in French these are "tous ceux qui habitent le territoire"). They should comply with constitutional laws setting main freedoms, rights and legal interests within definite legal confines (substantial requirement) and be officially published in accordance with a strict written procedure (formal requirement).

If this effect has not been given, these are not rules of law. They should not be observed either by the parties of private law relations or by law enforcers, because that law which is sovereign and inviolable is the product of legislation in any legal tradition (in particular, civil law, common law, Soviet law, Muslim law).

Do lawmakers enjoy unfettered liberty when drafting conflict of law rules? First, law, this powerful instrument of sovereign persons, has always remained in their hands. There is nobody above supreme power or authority of sovereign states. However, based on the principle of harmonious

---

[31] UK legislation illustrates this well. For example, the State Immunity Act, 1978, this act is enacted by the Queen's most Excellent Majesty, by and with the advice and consent of the Lords Spiritual and Temporal, and Commons, in this present Parliament assembled, and by the authority of the same.

coexistence of sovereign states, which are mutually dependent, no state may enact or execute rules resting on operation of foreign material law rules in breach of public interest of a state closely connected with private international law relations.

By way of illustration, look at the following rule: "if the provision of the foreign law to be applied in a certain case is openly contrary to the public order of Turkey, the said provision shall not be applied. Where it is deemed necessary, Turkish law shall be applied".[32] In the most general sense of this term, public interest is a specific idea of keeping away from what is not amenable to the nature of a particular community making it grow and prosper in the long run. And there is no better way to determine it than to address it to a people inhabiting this particular community. Because it is up to them to decide what makes them all grow and prosper under unique or specific conditions.

In a private international law sphere this issue is traditionally handled by supra mandatory or directly applicable rules of law (as the case may be). For this reason, the same act states that "…where the competent foreign law is applied, in cases which the provisions of Turkish law is directly applied in terms of scope of application and purpose of regulation, the mentioned provision will be applied".[33] Should a legislator in such a case check and examine foreign laws to preclude such breaches? They should not. When drafting conflict of law rules, the legislator should only consider who confers individuals or corporations with an aggregate of legal rights and duties and who extends jurisdiction over them. Only the law of this sovereign entity should govern. When the answer to this question is properly made, the rightful application of prescribed conflict of law principles may not be precluded by anyone on the ground of the public interest inherent to national regulation.

There is also a broad conception of the rule of law resting on the idea of the contract advanced in the theory of states and implying a non-legislative source of legal rules. For sure, this conception does not and actually cannot oppose to the narrow conception of rules of law. But it goes a little further from the premises of the narrow conception. The best explanation is that in the age of globalization characterized by deep uncertainty and changing economic circumstances, lawmaking powers are extended among other voluntary and involuntary functional organizations or groups of individuals

---

[32] See Art. 5 of the Turkish Act on Private International and Procedural Law, 2007, No. 5718 ("TAPIPL 2007").
[33] See Art. 6 of the TAPIPL 2007.

to frame regulations suitable for specific circumstances and ensure their proper observance by the relevant persons.

In this second (broader or extensive) sense it embraces prescriptions, orders and regulations passed by state and non-state international organizations acting with a sanction of states. Paying particular attention to the nature of these organizations, they may never advance specific interests of one particular permanent and well-organized group rather those common to a number of groups. And it seems to be evident that as soon as these groups usurp legislative powers of states, this may threaten their sovereignty and may be fatal for them and people that inhabit them. In this case it should always be remembered, that a state is a specific initially voluntary and strictly functional association of individuals resting on a peculiar coercive mechanism to secure observance of its prescriptions made impartially with a view to ensuring internal order and advanced communication among its members. Based on this reasoning, the use of a notion of "rule of law" in this broader approach is both dangerous and misleading.

In the answer to the question, why a broader meaning should not be given to a term "rule of law", it is worth noting what should be a fundamental attribute of law. That is the sovereign power of the peoples forming a distinct community and ruling all types of activity inside this community in a way to develop specific ideas found to be in their deeply rooted customs and traditions. And what deserves particular attention is that law is a very powerful instrument in the hands of those ruling all and any affairs inside separate well-organized groups of individuals. It shows expectations of these individuals in their socio-economic life and thus is characterized by peculiar force and effect.

Before we leave this discussion, there is another interesting point to be noted. A rule of law is a basic form in which law is expressed. It cannot embrace all juridical and quasi-juridical phenomena, which are intended to ensure internal order and advanced communication among members of a particular community. They have a different intrinsic rationale or reasoning evidencing the legal intention, which is independent of the subjective will, when the latter may never be characterized by impartiality.

May rules of law ever be replaced with some other instruments or means of social regulation to guide and control all types of the human activity inside a definite community? Fixed natural rules underlying human (positive) rules and governing all socio-economic phenomena in the best interests of communities may never be abandoned. Because that is the law of self-preservation of communities to provide for the regulation as long as the relevant communities will exist. In this public interest manifests itself. It is a specific sovereign idea of keeping away from what is not amenable to a nature and spirit of a particular community[34] makes it grow and prosper under peculiar circumstances.

Based on this reasoning, we may never expect replacement of open, written sovereign impersonal commands and authorizations with other prescriptions, orders and regulations, which may never have the same legal effect as legal rules, especially now when sovereign states as well-organized associations regain their voice and significance on many issues in the sphere of international law, which goes far beyond what is fair reasonable and expected by the legal community. The same is true with respect to a separate type of rules of law in national systems of law which are conflict of law rules.

We are in the age of the written law when all ordinances and regulations are given in a clear and precise written form as a result of the discovery and further common diffusion of one of the greatest arts, the art of writing. Written law is the law of a distinct community living in its unique forms comprising a great number of legal rules having a firm legal footing in sovereign powers of states. These are the powers of states grounded upon public interest as the substratum of all and any sovereign actions and reasoning. It is a very powerful instrument of communities' survival and therefore may never be completely uprooted. For that reason operation of conflict of law rules may not fall into disuse, except for cases when states close their borders for foreigners. In this latter case private international law will definitely be of no practical value and necessity.

Rules of law in general and conflict of law rules in particular transform numerous forms of the human activity from the category of fact to the category of law. This gives rise to definite private law rights and obligations, which are duly established, acknowledged and protected by sovereign states on a cross-border basis through annexation of rights of action to these rights until their very extinction.

This all forms two sides of law:
(1) an objective side depending on a supreme will of a people inhabiting a definite territory as well as

---

[34] In this respect, see the strong words of the Israel Proclamation of Independence, 1948: "...*the Land of Israel was the birthplace of the Jewish people. Here their spiritual, religious and political identity was shaped. Here they first attained to statehood, created cultural values of national and universal significance and gave to the world the eternal Book of Books...*".

(2) a subjective side of law manifesting itself in the voluntary or involuntary (occasional) human activity to a specific effect being sensitive for a state.

That is law as a generic term and its elements, including private international law as a separate field of law.

2. DISTINGUISHING MARKS OF PRIVATE INTERNATIONAL LAW OF CORPORATIONS

In the previous chapter I sought to show the essence and nature of private international law as a separate field in national systems of law. Now I would like to consider the essential and leading characteristics of private international law of corporations as a distinct legal institute characterized by a specific scope and a strictly set boundary inside a system of the given field of law.

The main forms discussed in this chapter will be the corporation as a special phenomenon, its nature and particulars of its constitution affecting its legal status as a subject of a private international law activity. It is mainly because of its particular role in sustainable growth of communities advancing security and socio-economic well-being of their individuals pursuing personal financial and other interests in a joint activity having a firm legal basis in the relevant legal system. This role consists in the arrangement of different purchase, sale, exchange, donation and other relations supporting states and requiring special terms of treatment. These are the terms distinct from that applicable to individuals that hold and run a corporation and resting on the idea of public interest.

Therefore, rather than looking at the law governing private law relations in general I will examine the law ruling a separate category of these relations arising from the intention of those individuals representing corporations to do business, own and use labour and property abroad. These are corporate and other relations closely connected with them, which owing to a specific character attributable to internationality are submitted to private international law, which deal with them based on ideas of legislative consent and comity expressed in the relevant legal rules and principles.

To be more specific, I would like to discuss attributes that distinguish private international law of corporations from other legal institutes of this field of law. In other words, I intend to examine "corporate" in private international law relations and "international" in corporate and other relations closely connected with them. And by defining distinguishing marks of private international law of corporations and its principles, to set a boundary by which this legal institute of private international law is severed from other major divisions of this field of law such as private international law of physical persons, things and obligations together composing a complete system of private international law in different states around the world.

Recognising these distinguishing marks and points of private international law of corporations is necessary both for jurists and practitioners of law. It extends our perception of corporate law as law, which produced a corporation as a separate legal phenomenon extremely valuable in both practical and theoretical senses. It also extends our perception of private international law of corporations, which recognized a foreign corporation (marked by a sign of national identity) as a subject of a commercial and non-commercial private law activity closely connected with more than one state not only with regard to the form but also material with the aim to extend opportunities of individuals in a private law sphere.

This means that under the laws of host states foreign corporations may do business in any form possible and thus exercise general, special or particular powers granted by home states to own property, to sue and be sued in the appropriate forum.

Admitting the objective of corporate freedom as individual freedom of those voluntary entering into a joint commercial and non-commercial activity, private international law plays a very important role to meet this end. It ensures recognition of this freedom on a broad extra-territorial basis by operation of conflict of law rules to this effect. And these rules do not fundamentally differ from one legal system to another unlike other legal rules in great measure highlighting national customs and traditions, but show a high degree of commonality between prevailing ideas of the relevant fields of law and jurisprudence accepted by all advanced systems of law.

Earlier in the book I have already pointed out that the main idea of private international law as a field of domestic law, and private international law of corporations as its distinct legal institute, is to ensure private and public rights and interests in the choice of law applicable to private law relations, which private and public corporations (sovereign states) enter into on a cross-border basis. And in this discussion we use a term "interest" in its traditional literal sense – as a subject about which one (an individual, a smaller or larger group of individuals) is concerned. This idea comes from the nature of states as a specific form of associations, the complexity of their composition and particulars of their relations with individuals. It is framed to ensure the balance of power and interests of states represented by public authorities and private interests of physical persons acting singly or jointly with others (corporations).

On this basis, private international law of corporations (like other legal institutes of the given field of law) is a pure practical development of both jurists and practitioners of law, in response to pressing needs of definite communities in predictable cross-border corporate and other relations closely connected with them. There should always be an equilibrium between these two parties to a social contract (states and individuals). The reason of this is that they may not exist apart from each other. *De jure* there is no state as a legal fiction - without individuals constituting it. And *de facto* there is no individual not subjected to any state, its power and law (in Latin - *ex lege*) as the world is divided into unequal parts (territories). In particular, in Europe these parts are governed by mutually dependent but still independent sovereign states in a manner initially given in the Westphalian model of the international legal order based on distinct but closely connected cultural, religious and institutional ties.

The natural principle of freedom underlies sovereign actions to which legal theory and practice ascribe different names in accordance with particular ideas in different legal traditions. No one may instruct how this freedom should be used with respect to other sovereign states, but it is not absolute or unfettered, because there are bonds of mutual dependence. Their actions rest on the following maxim *"quod tibi non vis fieri, alteri ne feceris"* which cannot be met halfway for the inevitable negative consequences of increasing constrains for those not observing it or observing it only in a formal manner or sense.

The reality is that states decide whether a thing is legal or not judging by precise and exact criteria reflecting their deeply-rooted customs and traditions. Besides these are states that using their supreme power confer rights and impose duties on those closely tied with them by bonds of nationality, domicile and residence (individuals and corporations), which in a legal theory and practice are called as subjects of law. That is national law and supreme power of one particular state. Once this issue is addressed, only states may decide over a juridical effect of exercising private law rights and interests of those entering into relations with cross-border impact. Based on this reasoning, the lawmaker should be inspired to ensure private and public rights and interests in the choice of law (and forum) applicable to private law relations by drafting new rules for the use of private and public subjects of law.

Private international law of corporations dealing with a peculiar legal phenomenon is characterized by a number of very clear and complete legal rules (principles), which pursue their own end and make up part of a system in which they are placed. These are directly applicable rules precluding the very problem of conflicts of corporate and other laws. These are conflict of law rules addressing all the issues concerning law applicable to:

(1) persons (natural and legal persons) entering into cross-border corporate and other relations closely connected with them;
(2) things (material/non-material) over which corporations and other persons (individuals and states acting in the non-sovereign quality) enter into private international law disputes;
(3) corporate and other obligations arising as an effect of the said private international law relations.

There are also rules addressing issues concerning appropriate jurisdiction in corporate and other cross-border disputes closely connected with them and rules on recognition of decisions made by foreign courts. Without them the choice of applicable law, would never be completed in a manner disregarding all and any constrains in cross-border movement of persons accompanied by transfer of goods, services, things and technologies.

Private international law of corporations is also characterized by a distinct method (depending on the nature of private international law relations mandatory or optional coordination).[35] This manner of dealing with legal and jurisdictional problems is employed in all cases of extension of:

(1) functionality of corporations delivering goods and services abroad; or
(2) their composition creating conflicting legitimate regulatory interests of sovereign states, closely connected with these services, activities and foreign direct and indirect investments.

To remove them, a number of steps is required: from allocation by the appropriate court of private law relations with a foreign element in a proper system of law to establishment of legal rights and obligations. This makes its (this method) application exceedingly difficult for those dealing with private international law disputes.

There may not be any other private law remedy. The method employed by this field of law does not bear a close resemblance with other methods of private law. It goes far from national law (jurisdiction) of a home state and deals with laws (jurisdictions) of other states with which private international law disputes brought to court are closely connected.

---

[35] A method initially is a device or a number of devices employed by competent persons in pursuance of a specific end. In our case it is purely practical rather theoretical. That is the conflict of law and forum regulation being in service of law enforcers when they deal with legal problems arising by the submission of cross-border corporate and other relations closely connected with them to two or more states. This method is complex and comprehensive at once, though its origination dates back to the twelfth century AD.

This narrows the definition of this method of private international law of corporations. It is a necessary process in the choice of law and jurisdiction for corporate and other relations closely connected with them, by which law enforcers take definite steps relying on concrete conditions of each particular private international law case placed in their hands for the assertion and establishment of corporate law rights and obligations. It consists in submission of private international law relations to a proper system of law and appropriate system of courts.[36] When considered in this broadest sense this method does not differ from that of private international law and, as is often the case, different subjective methods may be used by law enforcers. They relate to the purpose of this process, which is the beginning and the end of it.

The effect this method produces may be summarised as follows:

(1) the assertion of private international law rights and duties;
(2) non-extinguishment of rights to remedy through extension of limitation periods of the law of forum so far as it is set by *lex causae* if it does not run counter the public policy of the state of the forum;
(3) the precise nature of the issue as to which material law to apply to private law relations placed in the hands of a court;
(4) the settlement of legal and jurisdictional problems arising between states each time when parties of private international law relations are in dispute; and
(5) the advancement of a foreign practice of doing business in a predictable way for states acting in their capacity as sovereign associations of individuals and corporations as voluntary associations of individuals furthering common commercial or non-commercial goals.

If private international law of corporations is practical law giving a practical way out when a foreign element appears to be a cause of a conflict of laws and jurisdictions, an inevitable result of improper exercising of private international law relations would be to trigger a specific mechanism of its settlement. Nobody may stipulate the relevant cause of action in the sphere of private international law regulation based merely on theoretical rather empirical reasons when experience evidences of its non-existence. It is critical and unconditional at once. However, a theory teaches us to take into consideration these multiple causes of action in a specific way to elaborate specific legal approaches in this sphere.

Since every practical law represents a certain mode of action, private international law of corporations provides for actions, which are necessary to invoke private international law rights and obligations of corporations in

---

[36] These are the systems closely and substantially connected with these relations.

a manner conforming to a main aim and a true purpose of this legal institute. Means to accomplish this aim are limited. This legal institute may face problems in connection with a specific nature and constitution of a corporation mainly binding legal rules will apply to keep order inside a definite community.

Through these binding rules directing the conduct of the parties in a predictable way for states, order is perfectly attained. The reason is that corporations are kept as persons sometimes acting in a manner inconsistent with public policy, public security and public health and likewise may produce strange and unpredictable results for home and host states. Therefore we think that no more could be asked as to the use of mainly binding rules in the sphere of private international law regulation of corporate relations.

In defining the means to be employed in this or that sphere of socio-economic relations attention has to be paid, first, to sensitivity of these relations for sustainable development of a distinct community; second, to the main object and scope of regulation; third, to possible effect of the chosen means, whether they are able or unable to tackle problems arising in this respect. Hence it follows, that the main purpose of practical law is to elaborate and develop principles of certain practical value and utility. And the main purpose of private international law of corporations as a separate legal institute is to set conditions for harmonious growth of private law relations across borders of states. Taking into account the specific nature of corporations deriving both from the objective and subjective wills, this effect we may have this effect only within limits set by lawmakers as to the scope of private international law rights and obligations, forms, characteristics and legal effect of a cross-border activity.

This boundary, separating private international law of corporations from other legal divisions of private international law, may be traced with logical precision. However, it is also clear from what precedes above that we have not yet proved that private international law of corporations is a distinct structural element in the system of private international law characterized by delimitation of the subject matter and method of regulation. To distinguish private international law of corporations from other legal institutes of this field of domestic law means to show its formal attributes, peculiar terminological apparatus and specific principles, which are under the purview of this legal institute and to identify questionable points of this legal institute.

2.1. Formal attributes of private international law of corporations

Private international law is law framed to bring order to the activity of law enforcers ensuring public and private law interests when a prime problem faced is that of conflict of laws attributable to private law disputes with a foreign element. This issue is handled by conflict of law rules of the state of a forum, which form part of a particular field of law to which we advert each time when we need to know how a cross-border commercial and non-commercial activity of individuals or groups of individuals (including states acting in a non-sovereign quality) has to be governed, based on which material law rules. This has never been less important than other divisions of domestic law. As soon as we have this answer, a private international law dispute brought to court is dealt with by the relevant law enforcer as if it is initially subjected to one or another governing law.

These conflict of law rules settling private international law disputes are given in the relevant sources of law.[37] They emanate from the sovereign power or will of states and fall into the following four categories:

(1) purely national legal forms providing for conflict of law rules governing cross-border corporate relations and other relations closely connected with them (labour, investment etc.) as well as directly applicable rules and international jurisdiction rules;

(2) national legal forms providing for conflict of law rules formulated by international organizations and incorporated into a national legal system;

(3) international legal acts providing for uniform conflict of law rules directly applicable to private international law relations arising between corporations and other parties subjected to states that passed these acts;

(4) international legal acts providing for the uniform material law regulation of private international law relations arising between parties subjected to states that enacted these acts.

---

[37] In the present context, we mean a particular term "sources of private international law" rather than a general term of sources of law. For example, in England the latter term embraces case law, legislation as well as European law as primary statements of law. But private international law as a separate field of domestic law (common law, civil law, socialist, Muslim law etc.) may never be the product of individual mind of those charged with administration of law (judges). For the particular nature and character of private international law relations it deals with, causing conflicting regulatory interests of states, it is the product of legislation. In other words, private international law is nothing else than the product of cooperative efforts of those having a mandate from the sovereign states to legislate.

Legal acts made by those having a mandate to legislate in a private international law sphere, ensure sustainable growth of a cross-border socio-economic activity of members of distinct communities characterized by distinct territorial extent. They all express a true sense and spirit of private international law of corporations and thus deserve a very loyal and laborious study, which should not be confined solely to a literal text, which significantly varies depending on a state rather the main idea inspiring a legislator in each specific case.

Thus, they all provide for compulsory rules on submission of definite private international law relations to one particular law and jurisdiction to establish, maintain and protect certain private law rights and obligations and prevent application of any other law to these specific private law relations. Nevertheless, it is important to note that the first category of these forms (national ones) characterized by distinct national traditions and values prevails over the others. The reason for this is in the very idea of law as a good number of strictly structured and systematized rules consciously worked out by the national legislative organ of the sovereign state and advanced by the court practice to a predictable for a home state effect.[38]

Each separate legal act is closely connected with other legal acts passed by sovereign persons for the regulation of socio-economic relations arising inside a separate community. Depending on the nature of a legal act in which private international law rules are formulated we may determine general or special legal acts, because it is common practice that based on a subject of regulation they are not all general or all special. This means that some of them (general acts) cover the most essential private or public law issues in a way to construct a national law framework to which other rules (special acts) will be added for the entire regulation of the whole diversity and complexity of socio-economic relations.

As to special legal acts, originating from the operation of the same power and developing the main reasoning of a lawmaker to specific factual cases, these legal acts have a narrow subject and consequently a narrow scope of regulation. Special legal acts may never annul general legal acts,[39] rather coexist with them and operate in line with the following maxim: *lex specialis derogat generali.*

---

[38] For the evidence please refer, in particular, to Spanish legislation in which it is given that "...*legal rules contained in international treaties shall have no direct application in Spain until they have become part of the domestic legal system by full publication thereof in Spanish Official State Gazette*" (Art. 1 of SCC 2009).

[39] The same is true as to general legal acts.

When we speak of cross-border corporate relations and other relations closely connected with them and their regulation, the issue arises as to the nature of these relations and their legal (juridical) effect. May these relations be governed by general rules of law? Corporations derive from the coexistent objective and subjective wills to their formation. For this reason, special treatment distinct from that applicable to persons, who hold and run them, putting forward a special legal regime and effect of its application. Based on this argument, it is evident that special conflict of law rules and principles, taking into account the peculiar nature of corporations and substance of corporate law relations, will prevail over general ones. It is also evident that judges and other persons charged with the settlement of these specific cross-border corporate and other disputes closely connected with them will deal with them as per the form and substance in conformity with these special laws.

The objective classification of private international law sources rests on a nature and character of ruling in this specific legal sphere. But in authoritative works adding to the ever-growing body of the science of private international law we may find subjective classifications resting on assessment of practical efficiency of these legal acts (this means whether they are perfect, quasi-perfect and imperfect). Using the idea of conflict of law rules, that these are rules for delimitation of interests of different states in regulation of private law relations closely connected with more than one state, we may never subject legal forms in which they are expressed to these categories even for purely practical or theoretical purposes.

Considering private international law as a field of law, it is not difficult to see that it does not resemble any other field of national or international law. Private international law keeps its own subject and method, based on which private international law of corporations as its legal institute places corporations like any other subjects of law under the authority of competent law enforcers. They decide which law to apply to specific legal relations with their participation in order to provide adequate protection to certain private law rights and interests.

Thus, private international law of corporations subjects these relations on formation, reorganization, cross-border commercial and non-commercial activity, insolvency and termination of national and foreign corporations engaged in an interstate activity to a specific mechanism. It is called upon every time these private law relations, being closely connected with more than one state, are in dispute and as a result are brought to court. By the use of this mechanism private international law of corporations guides us in the settlement of a specific category of private international law disputes related to the formation, reorganization, cross-border commercial and non-commercial activity, insolvency and termination of corporations accompanied by distinct legal effect in each private law case brought to court.

For this reason private international law of corporations may be defined as a body of rules set by a sovereign person for law enforcers in order to resolve private international law disputes of national or foreign corporations in a way to meet public interests of this sovereign person by retaining its separate identity as well as interests of other states. More precisely, it is a body of rules specifically designed by sovereign states to cover all and any issues on formation, reorganization, cross-border commercial and non-commercial activity, insolvency and termination of national and foreign corporations, which may result in conflict of law problems brought to foreign or national courts for their further settlement.

Private international law disputes with participation of corporations are the raw material for the relevant regulation to be handled by judges or jurists. In all these disputes the first thing to be governed is the legal status and capacity, by which a corporation is recognised by a home state to enter into commercial and non-commercial relations on a cross-border basis. The first of its duties is the duty to be loyal to laws of a home state. Next are contractual and extra contractual duties arising from its activity.

This accordingly affects conflict of law regulation resting primarily on application of lex societatis. That is the conflict of law principle referring to a national law of a corporation. So, do cross-border corporate and other disputes arising between corporations or between corporations and other subjects of law have specific characteristics exerting distinct formal effect on the relevant legal institute, its construction and constitution?

When we speak of a corporation as a subject of a private international law dispute originating from its cross-border commercial and non-commercial activity, we think of a person with distinct rights and obligations conferred (imposed) by a home state and recognized by host states. This person *de jure* becomes a subject of private international law from the date when the court to which this particular dispute is brought decides that there is a strong element of internationality.[40] From this date a private international law dispute falls under a number of conflict of law rules set in national law forms and undertaking changes in response to new economic, social and

---

[40] *De facto* this person appears to be a subject of private international law from the date of entrance into cross-border corporate and other relations closely connected with them.

other circumstances. This proves a mutually dependent nature of subjective and objective sides of law taking different but closely connected forms.

The survey of private international law forms in advanced sovereign states shows that private international law of corporations currently exhibits clear traces of systematic arrangement covering all the issues from the very formation of a corporation through to its termination. This is traditionally explained by the growth of a cross-border corporate activity and the necessity to have a normative material tallying exactly with pressing economic and social needs. This normative material is carefully collected both by jurists and judges who in this sphere which may be termed a particularly sensitive for corporations, call in assistance of business communities to frame rules suitable for them. This systematic arrangement of private international law of corporations is consistent with the main trend in law. A legal thought has to develop and take new forms when necessary. For this reason we may view formulation and subsequent diffusion of new legal institutes showing us a new stage in development of legal consciousness in communities from which they gain more than lose.

However, it soon becomes clear that there is no structural element of the well-organized system of law, which may ever reasonably remain apart from all other structural elements of this system. And private international law of corporations is not the exception. Being a separate structural element of the relevant field of law, it is nevertheless closely connected with other elements of this system such as:

(1) private international law of physical persons dealing with legal status of individuals in their activity closely connected with two or more sovereign states;

(2) private international law of things concerned with the legal status of (foreign) property in cross-border private law deals; and

(3) private international law of obligations addressing all and any issues referring to contractual and extra contractual legal rights and obligations with cross-border impact.

This legal institute naturally extends itself to a sphere of other legal institutes of private international law in the search for proper law and appropriate jurisdiction to cross-border corporate relations and other relations closely connected with them as a main idea of private international law of corporations. All these divisions of private international law rest on the very same terminological framework. One part of these terms was borrowed from philosophy of law, to which usual meaning for distinct legal systems is given by this unique social science. Another part - from different fields of law. These are in particular corporate, civil law, private international law, labour law etc. The reasoning connected with this is readily apparent. We may never grasp law as a mere number of fragmentary ordinances rather a system of fundamental rules and principles supplementing each other based on distinct combinations of terms implemented by legislation or recognized/sanctioned by courts.

2.2. Terminological apparatus of private international law of corporations

We cannot proceed with a study of issues justifying a separate position of private international law of corporations in the relevant field for law without analysing its terminology. Private international law has always been a complex field of national law and an uncertain field of jurisprudence, dealing with the elimination of theoretical and practical constrains when exercising private law rights on a cross-border basis. It rests on specific firmly-rooted historical, cultural, religious and other customs and traditions manifested in their jurists and judge-made law and therefore is filled with terms and notions having distinct meaning and playing diverse roles in different states depending on the time, place and circumstances. And when we analyse these terms and notions advanced by the theory of law and employed by distinct systems of law, we need to accept that these are theoretical reflections having a particular practical value when resolving such separate legal problems as conflicts of laws and conflicts of jurisdictions. They will be illustrated in each particular case later.

To begin with, national law terms and notions lead back to definite historic, cultural and legal development of a particular community. Their aims are different from those identifying the essence of private international law relations to those showing ways out of specific conflicts of law and jurisdiction problems arising in corporate and other spheres. And consequently they have a particular value in public and private law spheres of regulation of socio-economic relations within a definite community.

The main role of private international law of corporations generally consists in resolution of private international law disputes of corporations with physical and legal persons (including states), which they bring to competent persons of states in order to reassert their legal status and establish and defend private law rights and obligations. In this and other parts of this book a private international law dispute is a matter of a real, significant and good faith controversy between the parties to a contract or arising beyond the bounds of a contract over private law rights and obligations (their cause, particulars of the use and effect) submitted to two or more separate legal orders.

The true aim of the private international law of corporations is to produce theories and doctrines based on principles comparable to those of natural to facilitate a cross-border activity of national and foreign corporations in the interests of particular states. The terminology for this, taking into consideration their private law nature does not have a uniform meaning across the world. Nevertheless, this does not preclude the assemblage of these terms in the present book.

Some of these terms were borrowed from the general philosophy of law, another from different fields of law (corporate and civil law) giving rise to a complex aggregate of rights and obligators necessary for participation in cross-border corporate and other relations closely connected with them. They are brought together here in order to show the complexity of the subject matter, to avoid mingling of distinct national conceptions expressed in rules of law.

The term "corporation" is the first and principal term behind a number of these ideas of the given legal institute in each distinct system of law. Through the recorded history we know that sovereign states have long assigned a clear and precise idea to a corporation responding exactly to pressing needs of the socio-economic development of a community. Besides, it is well noted that at all times the main idea of a corporation was to extend financial potential of incorporators,[41] economic potential of states and ensure social protection of individuals,[42] being nationals of states through the proper use of private and public property and enjoyment of specific corporate rights conferred by sovereign states. These are rights of individuals to contract a specific legal status proceeding from competent authorities. But that is not the only meaning of this term.

Depending on the end of a particular survey undertaken by researchers, different meaning may be ascribed to this term. For economists it is a powerful tool when constructing steady and harmonious socio-economic relations of the time and place. For politicians a corporation is a perfect means to attain certain political goals. For sociologists it is an integral part of the social fabric of a particular well-organized group. For judges it is a separate subject of law and a distinct subject of private law relations having

---

[41] These are individuals acting singly or jointly with others, whose names are subscribed to the relevant memorandum of a private law association or any other act prescribed by applicable law. That is law of the place of incorporation.

[42] Corporations contribute to national treasuries of home states much sums as taxes and other payments to fund governments to solve pressing socio-economic needs of the time and place.

a particular value for sovereign states. For jurists it is an association of individuals having a legal personality distinct from them.

These are approaches taken by economic, political, social and legal theories of corporations to characterize this phenomenon in the most general or abstract sense in accordance with a method of broad analogies employed by them in these distinct socio-economic spheres. For this very reason they cannot be of any use in our legal research requiring unequivocal and capacious formulations of all terms.

As far as the term "corporation" is concerned, when we consider it as a tool or a specific means to attain one's goals, it appears that we reduce the role which corporations play for individuals and communities in general framing their socio-economic activities. Certainly, we have no reasons for this belief. It also means that we reduce the role of individuals thus subjecting them to operation of a mechanical theory, which comes to be predominant in this sphere, which should always be avoided by all possible means. Likewise, corporations should not be dealt with in theory and practice in the same way as machines are dealt with by operators. A corporation has always meant more than a mere tool. By a corporation we understand a form of a voluntary association of individuals joining their skills, experience and property to further one common goal under a separate name. However, this is not the only way to perceive it.

To define a corporation means to show main attributes, specific marks and points of this particular social, economic, political and legal phenomenon. Therefore we may regard a corporation as a form of a voluntary association of individuals characterized by limited liability and shared property, to which a home state concedes (and host states recognize) a separate legal capacity to exercise its free will over things and actions to make profit or attain any other legally enforceable common end (objective) under a separate name. This definition of the term corporation clarifies its nature and substance for further use in legal theory.

The reader may observe that this notion is part empirical, and part theoretical. The reason of this rests on the fact that a corporation is a product of law, which as far as it is concerned is a synthesis of theory and practice. And it would be unfair to disregard this detail, because corporations strictly correspond to separate conceptions framed by sovereign states to themselves to have what they are really interested in, keeping in mind specific time, place and circumstances exercising much influence upon all things and actions in this material world. Thus far whatever idea we form of a corporation, it is the one based on theory and practice appropriate for the specific time, place and circumstances and marked by appropriate peculiarities.

Going deeper, all corporations are independent subjects of law acting based on definite material law principles peculiar to sovereign states and their unique deeply rooted legal traditions. Their composition and functionality varies along many lines depending on a subjective will of individuals. However, what always remains unaltered is a nature of corporations. They originate from objective interests of states and subjective interests of individuals to the effect to give rise to a separate legal person with a definite scope of rights and obligations in a socio-economic sphere and characterized by limited liability, shared property and a specific system of governance.

Thus, corporations are a product of the time brought into being in response to pressing economic, political, social and legal needs of communities. As soon as all these needs are met, there probably will not be any need for corporations as separate subjects of law. Now we need to clarify what constitutes the main attribute of being in such a capacity of the subject of law, which makes corporations enter into legal transactions of a commercial (industrial, financial, professional etc.) and non-commercial (e.g. social) character. Hence, the next term to be considered in the present part of the paper shall be "legal personality".

In the most general signification of this term, a legal personality is a scope of rights, duties and responsibility conceded by a home state to persons (physical or juridical/legal). However, I do not want to reduce the notion of a corporate personality as a separate type of a legal personality to a number of rights and duties, as well as responsibility conferred (imposed) by states to a voluntary and functional association of individuals in order to put it into a legal state of a subject. I prefer to consider this term in different senses, which may be of some theoretical and practical value for a reader.

Thus in the theoretical sense a legal personality is a capacity for legal action inducing rights, correlative obligations and responsibility. In a practical sense, a legal personality is a sum of rights supported by corresponding duties and responsibility for their good faith enjoyment in different socio-economic spheres of the relevant community. It is sufficiently recognized that it puts legal persons in the same legal position as physical persons. And going a little deeper, evidencing a peculiar nature of corporations deriving from legal enactment, it is inextricably linked with home states suggesting a special statutory mode of conferring particular legal status.

In the sphere of conflict of law regulation these states are otherwise known as states of corporate nationality. At this observation we would like to point out that there should not be any confusion as to corporate personality and nationality of corporations (in French - *nationalité des sociétés*). These are two different legal categories having their own ideas and means to achieve them. Nevertheless, they are closely connected in the private international law sphere. The reason is evident – there is no corporation if it is not subjected to a definite state, which is its home state. Besides if physical persons may have double or multiple nationality, corporations may never have it. The point is that these are persons existing due to operation of law. And only law gives rise to separate subjects of law characterized by specific organs, through which they may act, confer rights and duties, sue and be sued.

Nevertheless, corporate nationality is more than a mere corporate location of business. It is loyalty and commitment of those constituting a corporation to a particular state conferring them with a distinct number of legal rights, duties and responsibility in order to deal freely in commercial and non-commercial spheres of a socio-economic life of the relevant community as one party. And finally with complete extinguishment of the corporate personality granted by a home state, these are no longer corporate bodies needing any nationality.

Next, we would like to consider a term "corporate property" having a particular significance in the corporate law sphere dealing with specific legal phenomena. Under this term we mean a complex of material and non-material things (including intellectual property rights) exclusively held by a corporation, to which they were given by individuals acting singly or jointly with others to pursue one common end, or acquired by a corporation at its corporate activity.[43] This is due to the fact that a corporation would never be treated as a subject of law rather a mere fiction without having means to ensure its duties and bear responsibility. These are duties and responsibility severable from those of incorporators and a home state itself for the corporate property found to be in the structure of a corporation to maintain its distinct status of a subject of law. This exclusive holding of property is evidenced by constitutional documents of a corporation owing to the fact that a corporation is a product of the sovereign will of a people inhabiting a distinct territory appearing in the relevant legal enactment.

---

[43] Thus, participation in this form of a voluntary and functional association of individuals advancing a common idea or specific end of the joint activity exerts much influence on individual property. Besides it should always be remembered that corporate property is not all individual property of those entering into a joint corporate activity rather the one specifically transferred to the ownership or exclusive possession of a corporation. This property serves the main end of the joint corporate activity of individuals.

Having considered the term "corporation" and other terms closely connected with it, it is time to examine the core of theoretical apparatus of private international law of corporations. That is the term "private international law relations". Private international law has always been national law. It is distinct from international law developed by unions of sovereign states and international institutions to advance ideas common for all states or their most part. It uses the language belonging to particular communities and reflecting their distinct legal expectations and experience as to settlement of problems arising between:

(1) conflicting systems of law when deciding, which system is closely and substantially connected with private international law relations for the further governance; and

(2) conflicting jurisdictions when addressing the issue, which court should hear and determine private law disputes with foreign elements.

And it is sufficiently recognized that these private law disputes with foreign elements or private international law relations form a subject matter of the distinct field of law (private international law), which cannot be properly understood without clearly defined terms.

For this very reason we pay particular attention to this term as well as the term "private international law", which in this book is used with reference to a system of duly formulated and properly fixed legal rules and principles governing private law relations with a cross-border dimension from the choice of appropriate jurisdiction and proper law to enforcement of foreign court judgments in a manner acceptable for a particular community.[44] And when speaking of "proper law" and "appropriate jurisdiction" in the present context we mean a system of law and a system of courts having an overwhelmingly closer connection with private international law relations. To respond to this test this connection with one particular state and jurisdiction should become overwhelmingly stronger than any other one based on a number of factors to be considered later herein.

---

[44] For an excellent illustration of this point of view see art. 1 of Private International Law Code of the Republic of Tunisia, 1998 ("PILC 1998"), in which it is given that *"les dispositions de ce code ont pour objet de déterminer pour les rapports privés internationaux:*

1 - La compétence judiciaire des juridictions tunisiennes.

2 - Les effets en Tunisie des décisions et jugements étrangers.

3 - Les immunités juridictionnelles et d'exécution.

4 - Le droit applicable".

The subject matter of the field of legislation should not be confused for the one of the relevant field of law. But in this particular case they coincide.

So far by the term "private international law relations" we mean legal relations as they are found to be established between definite persons (corporations, individuals and states) on a cross-border basis by their deliberate or voluntary or undeliberate and involuntary actions (contractual and extra contractual relations) as the case may be. Practically speaking, that is the exchange of private rights and obligations on a cross-border basis in a contractual or extra contractual form with a certain material or non-material effect for the parties involved. If exercised wrongly, these relations cause particular problems named in the private international law "conflicts of laws".

It is argued that when there is no dispute as to laws or national legislation on civil law issues[45], there is no conflict of laws. I agree with this, but not entirely. In the private international law sphere there is a special conflict, which is a logical consequence of improper implementation by private law subjects of their cross-border relations, when at the settlement of their disputes laws of two or more states need to be taken into account through subjective or objective connections with these relations. What falls within this term "conflict of laws", when harmonious coexistence of different national laws is presumed, based on sovereignty, freedom, independence and equality of states with common rights and obligations under law of nations?

Determining the exact meaning of this term "conflict of laws" requires showing its specific content as to the origin and main purpose of private international law. If considered this way, conflict of laws is a collision of public law interests or confrontation of laws over the ruling of private law relations burdened with a foreign element, when law enforcers are asked which state has a legitimate regulatory interest in a private law relation.

As it may be seen in this and other notions employed in the private international law sphere there is a permanent element. That is a "foreign element", which does not have a normative definition,[46] though it is perfectly

---

[45] In the present context we refer to civil law as the mother of all fields of private law, be it corporate, commercial, trade, banking, investment and any other field law advanced in national systems of law (civil, common etc.).

[46] Save for the Law of Ukraine on Private International Law, 2005 No. 2709-IV (as amended on 3 November 2016), in which a foreign element is defined as a sign characterizing private law relations submitted to this Law and taking one or several following forms: at least one participant of private law relations is a foreign national, a stateless person or a foreign legal entity; the subject matter of private law relations is placed abroad; the legal fact creating, changing or terminating private law relations took or takes place abroad.

given in a doctrine of private international law treating it as a legal phenomenon, which may never be the same. The point is that reference to this term is made in the enormous legislative and court practice.

Thus, for instance, the Turkish legislator when determining the scope of private international law regulation provides that "this Act regulates the law applicable to private law transactions and relations that contain a foreign element…".[47] Because it is not a mere idea rather reality posing different questions, which are not easy to answer. And that is the one which "founding fathers of private international law" faced when handling the problem of the first conflict of laws.[48]

That is the element having no connection with a legal system governing other elements of private law relations but being of a true practical value for the nature and effect of distinct private law relations. Because it exerts a significant influence on the litigation (its process and effect). Therefore, there are different formulas of conflict of law rules, devising ways to deal with it in a manner acceptable for the community closely and substantially connected with these relations.

Thus far in a doctrinal or scientific sense conflict of laws means a collision of rights and legitimate regulatory interests of two or more states in the ruling of private law relations arising between different subjects of law (physical, legal persons and even states acting in a non-sovereign quality), which judges for the assertion of private law rights and obligations place them in the hands of those where there is controversy in their implementation. Keeping in mind that these are laws in a private law sphere, it should be noted that the problem of a conflict is settled by specific means. These are directly applicable rules and conflict of law rules. Separate but closely connected with them are rules on international jurisdiction indicating territorial settlement of conflicts of laws as well as scope and extent of jurisdiction over private international law disputes brought to court. This entails submission of private law relations with a foreign (international) element to definite law and jurisdiction with which these relations are closely connected and which extend their force over a separate territory.

---

[47] See Art. 1 of the TAPIPL 2007.

[48] A peculiar nature of private international law should always be taken into consideration. In its fundamentals private international law is nothing else than written law or rules-based law. For this reason when referring to the settlement of the problem of conflicting interests of states we address this issue by the use of the relevant conflict of law principles set by sovereign states in the relevant legal sources rather customs and traditions falling under the category of law of merchants (or in Latin - *lex mercatoria).*

Another issue arises when laws which normally operate in coexistence come into conflict. This is not a conflict of earlier and later enacted national law acts or a conflict of general and special laws to which we referred earlier in the present paper, but a conflict of material laws of different sovereign states. Only material law rules may be in conflict. It seems to be evident that the issue may never be raised with respect to procedural and technical rules because they are strictly territorial and may not be applied by foreign courts and other institutions charged with settlement of private international law problems except for specific cases, which will be considered later. And the only key to settling conflict of law problems is a conflict of law rule laid down in the relevant national private international law act.

Next I intend to pay particular attention to terms common for all legal institutes of private international law, which in each specific case may have a different role and meaning in the system of this field of law. In the present context it may be useful to remind the reader that private international law has always been regarded as a field of law dealing with a problem of conflicting systems of law arising in private law disputes with a "foreign element" or a number of foreign elements.

In accordance with its ordinary usage a foreign element means a constituent part of private law relations (subjective or objective depending on a case) submitted to two or more separate public orders. As soon as each element of private law relations is traditionally submitted to separate public order, this foreign (or sometimes even termed "international") element is foreign for a state, to which court a separate private law dispute is brought and thus should be considered with the meaning attached to it by a home state. For this reason it is obvious that a foreign element is a distinctive and indispensable mark of private international law as a separate field of private law in each state and jurisdiction.

In the most extensive signification of this term, a foreign element is the main reason of subjection of private law relations to two or more distinct legal orders. It should be noted that this subjection to different legal orders is a pure matter of fact, which *should not* give rise to a separate legal idea. Nevertheless, this idea arises. And it is interesting to know, what this idea rests upon.

When dealing with this issue we need to know the scope and content of the term "legal idea" or better "idea of private law". There has always been much discussion in the past over what this idea of private law is. Private law relations have long been regarded as purely national relations resting on territorial operation of law. These private law relations (as a subjective side of law) proceeded upon national material law principles predictable for the parties (an objective side of law). And this accordingly affected operative rights of those entering into them. Nevertheless, with state borders left open to foreigners this operation of law became extraterritorial. The rights of individuals, being a subject matter of conscious observation, were extended far beyond borders of states in which they originated and were correspondingly recognized by host states subject to definite limitations.

This has essentially affected material law principles governing these relations. But that is the second issue, the first one is what this idea of private law is. That is the governing idea of sovereign states translated into specific terms and concepts in their national law reflecting national customs and traditions. Its peculiarity is brought out by the use of specific private law forms and institutions complying exactly with a legal tradition to which an enacting state belongs. It seems to be evident that private law is law exerting much influence upon the will and volition of individuals connected with states by bonds of nationality, domicile or permanent residence. Therefore it has always been very important to point out the relation of this idea to a legal thought and thus consider the effect of this law, which may be of the utmost social influence. The meaning of this term has not greatly varied from the date of its origination. From the very origination it is clear and precise. In modern theory and practice it is perceived as the main legal category of private international law generating numerous legal phenomena.

The term "foreign element" deserves to be respected for its particular role in theory and practice of private international law regulation. The idea of a foreign element has been commonly formulated and developed in all civilized states and therefore no problem ever arose as to its equal treatment in different national fora. This foreign element is "seated" as an integral part in all legal relations subjected to directly applicable rules, conflict of law rules and international jurisdiction rules comprising private international law from the very commencement until their cessation. To be more definite, its mere presence in the structure of disputed private law relations, causes operation of a specific mechanism dealing with legal and jurisdictional problems in the private international law sphere. This necessarily implies application of directly applicable rules, conflict of law rules and international jurisdiction rules to private law relations. Otherwise, private international law would remain silent on the governance of these relations.

2.3. On right and wrong principles in private international law of corporations

Private international law may be defined as certain and evident knowledge of the means to solve the multiplicity of legal and jurisdictional problems arising in the private law sphere when there is a foreign element present in the structure of commercial and non-commercial private law relations. However, this knowledge, being a purely subjective philosophical category, is not free from false ideas, which need to be identified and rebutted for the further development of a classical type of positive law, to ensure effective communication between communities and their members.

To meet this end proper terminology adequately showing modern socio-economic problems as well as methodology furnishing proper legal instruments to this effect should be used. With this in mind we need to establish the conformity of rules and principles employed by private international law of corporations with the general idea of a subject of law[49] and a specific idea of a corporation as a subject of private international law (when considered in isolation) and private international law relations (when viewed dynamically).

Private international law of corporations as a practical legal institute dealing with extremely complicated corporate law issues "seated" in distinct legal orders cannot steadily develop with the use of weak or wrong premises. Its regulation strongly affects public interests of sovereign states closely connected with cross-border corporate and other disputes arising in this sphere. There is nothing more dangerous than subjection of private law rights in the corporate law sphere to improper law or jurisdiction. This may trigger retortions cynical disregard of sovereign rights of others over private international law issues dominating over national ones.

For this reason the main maxim for lawmakers and enforcers in this sphere should be that to ensure unerring application of law and jurisdiction by all possible means in both public and private law interests. And when evaluating and comparing interests of states and individuals in the proper settlement of legal and jurisdictional problems, the interests of states will always prevail. It is generally understood and universally accepted that sovereign states further interests of their peoples as the only bearers of sovereignty, and in accordance with these interests also interests of other states (be they neighbouring or not) should be duly followed especially now when there are practically no obstacles to cross borders of foreign countries for whatever practical reasons (tourism, business, science and so forth).

This nevertheless does not mean that these public interests should go against private interests of individuals comprising distinct communities. Under

---

[49] Using the term a "subject of law" we mean also a "subject of power", which is supreme power of the relevant state. For this very reason there is a set dichotomy – subject of national and foreign law or national and foreign subject of law.

these circumstances there should not be anything inconsistent with the main idea of corporate law and private international law as well as a specific idea of private international law of corporations resting on pure practical reasons. These are unerring choice of applicable law and jurisdiction accompanied by enforcement of decisions made by foreign courts with respect to corporations as a peculiar legal phenomenon.

To illustrate the essential principles underlying the above-mentioned activity of makers and enforcers of private international law of corporations, are divided into two main groups:

- material law principles deriving from the general concept of subjects of law and those to be found in the specific nature and character of corporations uncovering the true mechanism of their operation and placing corporations on a firm legal ground;

- conflict of law principles[50] and international jurisdiction principles dependent on a specific nature and essence of corporations and protecting their interests as well as interests of their incorporators and third parties entering into cross-border relations with them.

This short classification of leading principles to be found in national legislation of distinct sovereign states is not comprehensive. Nevertheless, the principles are accurately and specifically defined in legal theory and practice in separate states and do not need a separate explanation for the inherent completeness in themselves.

All these principles are characterized by the same source, brought into law through the use of a number of simple and complex logical operations. They are also distinguished by a complex of legal consequences predictable for sovereign states and private law subjects as to a peculiar subject of regulation. That is a corporation as a subject of private international law when considered in isolation and a subject of private international law relations when viewed dynamically.

2.3.1. Multinational corporations

There is a set of legal principles, which completely leave out:
(1) a specific nature of corporations deriving from sovereign states and their laws;

---

[50] These are 1) *lex societatis* determining the legal status of a foreign corporation as a subject of commercial and non-commercial transactions on a cross-border basis, 2) *lex personalis* dealing with legal rights and interests of consumers entering into specific private law relations with corporations on a cross-border basis, 3) *lex rei sitae* concerned with the legal status of corporate property placed abroad.

(2) their peculiar strictly functional essence consisting in the extension of freedom of individuals furthering one common legally enforceable objective within socio-economic spheres of distinct communities initially presenting high risks for them; and

(3) their ultimate purpose to serve interests of home states.

We are speaking of principles relating to multinational corporations and relying on a new corporate law framework freed from national law bounds. Many contemporary researchers support them as a panacea against all modern economic problems, which cannot be settled by traditional national law forms and institutions undergoing multiple refinements to respond to socio-economic concerns of the time and place. It seems that these principles are produced by a mercantile legal thought directed to satisfy large business interests and rest solely on subjective ideas.

Since these ideas are inherently void of impartiality, these principles should be avoided by all those dealing with a corporation as a subject of law, being under the purview of corporate law, and a subject of private international law relations, which legal status is governed by private international law of corporations. For a further proof let us have a look at issues as to:

(1) what ideas national or so called "multinational" corporations are equipped with;

(2) on which conditions these ideas were set; and

(3) whether these ideas explain the origin and historical and socio-economic specificities of development of corporations as a peculiar legal phenomenon.

Through the recorded history we know that a corporation is a unique legal, economic and even political phenomenon regardless of the place of rendering services or making works. This uniqueness consists in that fact that a corporation is intrinsically a specific idea born in minds of legislators and supported by other persons charged with personification of what intrinsically cannot have any personality.

It takes the form of people acting on behalf of a corporation and property legally held by a corporation in a specific form, which through resting unchanged for many centuries explain the origin and socio-economic specificities of this legal phenomenon development. However, through successful operation of this idea based on a peculiar method and a form of personification we all know that even if we do not see it, it is formed and continues to exist until the date stipulated by the legislator or persons holding it (date of complete extinguishment of the corporate personality). And it does not matter whether a corporation enters into international commerce or not to meet this aim. It never becomes foreign simply because it does business abroad.

That is what we call a corporation. It is nothing else than a form of a voluntary association of individuals characterized by limited liability and shared property, to which a home state concedes (and host states recognize) a separate legal capacity to exercise its free will over things and actions to make a profit or attain any other legally enforceable common end (objective) under a separate name.

Its uniqueness at all times rested on results of scientific and technological progress, which were perfectly implemented in models of national corporate law forms for the benefit of a private as well as a public law spheres of a socio-economic activity. Respecting the idea of a corporation, it has invariably embraced different legal phenomena as the most recent developments of legal theory and practice. These are in particular: 1) legal personality of a corporation; 2) nationality of a corporation; 3) limited liability of incorporators, which may keep this form of associations abreast of the time with its social, economic and political challenges. And ones granted (legal personality) or assumed (nationality of a corporation and limited liability of incorporators) by a home state no one may change it.

With this in mind let us try to answer the question as to what is an objective criterion for distinguishing national and multinational corporations, which is very important for us. It is also important to show, whether this distinction (if any) is reasonable. For this we should study the essence of corporations, paying particular attention to their attributes. This is invariably investigated along many lines of questions as to what makes a corporation.

First, a corporation is solely premised on the idea of a private law association. That is an association of individuals transferring their individual property to a corporation they form in order to reach some common end in commercial or non-commercial spheres inside a definite community jointly. Second, this idea of a private law association in its turn is premised on the idea of individual freedom of those voluntary entering into a joint commercial and non-commercial activity by operation of law, this powerful but purely national regulatory instrument characterized by sovereignty extending over a definite territory. This individual freedom is not absolute. It is limited by legal categories of rights and duties supported by a specific legal category of responsibility. Third, this freedom has different meanings in separate states thus affecting the scope of rights, powers, privileges and obligations of corporations as subjects of law (nationals of the relevant states).

Corporations may never have double or multiple nationality. It is sufficiently recognized that corporations may not have any inherent rights by themselves. Nevertheless, these are subjects of private law. That is law expressed in national rules of law, including conflict of law rules having limited territorial application. Otherwise this would be against a specific nature of corporations, which are accountable to a separate state and its jurisdiction on all and any issues of their corporate life by a mere fact of incorporation, which is nevertheless very important.

As to consequences of double or multiple nationality for states and third parties, it has to be said that the paradigms of private law and international law have to undergo cardinal changes. In the present state we may never have legal persons with double or multiple legal personality and as a result corporations with double or multiple nationality for the sound foundation, on which the rationale of corporate law rests. That is the theory of corporations premised on another operative theory, which is the theory of legislation resting on supremacy and inviolability of law made by competent national authorities.[51]

Advancing the idea of certainty in a private law sphere this theory of corporations develops deductively all consequences of the relevant legal principles operating in a manner to ensure a particular practical value of the study of corporate law in the governance of a separate type of socio-economic relations arising inside a community. Furthermore, this theory convincingly refutes both double/multiple nationality and missing nationality of corporations as running counter the underlying legal policy of sovereign states.

This policy is grounded upon the idea that the activity of corporations is accompanied by certain risks which their representatives (employees, executives etc.) bear while carrying it on in whichever place possible within fields of activities assigned to them. Taking this into account, double or multiple nationality of corporations are phenomena unknown and unacceptable for law, those public and private law interests, being backed by law.[52] Their operation may be *la source de tout désordre* (in French) for unpredictability of:

---

[51] This idea of law has traditionally been neatly fixed in the text of constitutions. For example, in Syria, *"the supremacy of law is a fundamental principle in the society and the state"* (See the text of C 1973).

[52] For a more objective view see Bill S. 1876, introduced in the Senate of the United States on 14 May 1971 by Mr Burdick, which states that *"a corporation incorporated by more than one territorial jurisdiction shall be deemed to be a citizen only of one of those*

(1) law governing the form and content of this type of the joint activity of individuals (a corporate activity) as well as a general effect of this law application;

(2) appropriate jurisdiction and its effect;

(3) legal consequences for home states and third parties.

However, this does not mean that a corporation may not change its nationality when this right is conferred by a state of initial incorporation and recognized by a state of reincorporation.[53] Based on law of continuity advanced in corporate law as a relevant field of law in national systems of law this freedom of reincorporation is kept among the main private law freedoms in different states. Nevertheless, this is not the case, which we would like to consider in detail in the present context.

There are so many legal definitions of a multinational company, which I cannot leave without expressing my personal view supported by a firm argument, using the Cartesian method of systematic doubt. This method gives us reasons to conclude that it is a fallacy to talk or think of multinational corporations in a way apart from a national legal framework as the mother of all legal forms and institutions.

A multinational corporation is nothing other than a group of national corporations set up in different states and jurisdictions for different goals and conducting their separate corporate activity across borders of one state. Hence, it means that it is neither a new form nor a new type of corporation rather a group of corporations of different nationality united by a common end. If we reach this conclusion, we should reject this term and relevant notions given by jurists in support of their position comme entachés du doute (if using the French language), resting on the authority and autonomy of reasoning other than the objective one. Consequently from the point of law so-called "multinational" corporations are nothing else than a fiction. For this reason we cannot place a confusing definition of multinational corporations among notions, which come within the scope of terminological apparatus of private international law of corporations and do not raise doubts or controversies.

---

jurisdictions that will establish diversity of citizenship between the corporation and a party adverse to it…" (Para 2375).

[53] For a more objective view see Art. 19 of the Polish Act on Private International Law, 2011 ("PAPIL 2011") *"…after the seat of the moral person has been moved to another country, the moral person shall be subject to the law of this country since the moment of the transmission…".* This will be the state of corporate nationality.

This means that all these contemporary legal principles rest on the end of corporations and therefore fall apart upon examination of their nature and essence. However, there is a very important issue to note. Legal reality is grounded upon definite postulates, which just serve economic needs. Law does not serve economic reality rather builds, preserves and augments a socio-economic life of well-organized permanent groups of individuals in a predictable for these groups manner in the long run. And in advanced states the choice of legal terms is traditionally made very intelligently.

That is the main idea being put forward in the present section in line with the one that lawmaking should invariably be kept far from functional associations of states and other international organizations. Just think what this would mean were it really true: these private law associations would be out of state control. And thus holding considerable funds they may easily destroy states, when they advance their own interests rather interests of states. These are sovereign interests of individuals comprising these states especially in the issue of replacement of a national corporate law framework premised on traditional doctrines, with an international one, which constitutes a real threat to these states.

In theory and practice of conflict of law regulation in different states we may find both right and wrong rules and principles. From a practical point of view false or weak principles are those, which do not render possible proper furtherance of the end of private international law – allocation of legal relations with a foreign element in the proper system of law and jurisdiction. Therefore they should never be used. But this does not mean that we should not consider them in view of the fact that at all times this motivates the refinement of right principles.

Having addressed the issue of the use of right and wrong principles in the sphere of regulation of cross-border corporate law relations, it thus should be clear enough that private international law of corporations is not a legal institute that will adopt wrong principles as maxims underlying the activity of those dealing with exceedingly complicated legal and jurisdictional problems of the time and place, because it is dangerous, taking into view a particular character of ruling in this sphere, which rests on the idea of public interest intrinsic to all and any law enforcing activity carried out in this respect.

2.4. On questionable points of private international law of corporations

In the preceding section I have expounded the idea of right and wrong principles and their role in private international law of corporations. Now I would like to outline of questionable issues of this separate legal institute of private international law in national systems of law. It requires more skills and knowledge from all those charged with this specific type of regulation in order to preclude their inability, disinterest and blindness when resolving complicated legal issues.

These are issues that law enforcers face when dealing with conflict of law problems arising at the settlement of cross-border corporate and other disputes closely connected with them. In practice, law enforcers face numerous contingencies when considering corporate, labour, investment and other private international law disputes to which they have to be duly prepared. Hopefully, this list is not too long. Among critical ones are different formulas employed by the very same conflict of law principles and their distinct application in national fora.

This difference arises because of distinct guiding principles contained in all these formulas reflecting public interests of states in the appropriate sphere of socio-economic relations. In other words, different national ideas are attached to these conflict of law principles though the same value is given to them by states. These are public interests, which take distinct legal forms based on autonomy of objective and impartial sovereign reasoning.

These forms create contrasting results when arriving at the settlement of private international law disputes in distinct national law fora. We may never hope to choose legal forms common for all communities because it is simply impossible. The reason is evident, we may never have unity in this particularly sensitive sphere of socio-economic regulation (private international law sphere) resting on the idea of supremacy and inviolability of law, which is a purely national development. At the same time, we may never assume absolute independence of states in making and enforcing rules to deal with legal and jurisdictional problems arising in the corporate sphere with cross-border impact.

For this reason we need to show these formulae and make clear what ideas are behind them in order to ensure legal certainty necessary for individuals to foresee positive and negative consequences of all and any corporate law actions with cross-border impact. For example, there are different criteria, when determining personal law of corporations for the purpose of conflict of law regulation in the corporate law sphere.

Practice shows that states advance distinct determinants with respect to the choice of law to apply to a wide range of corporate law issues burdened with foreign elements and govern the substance of cross-border corporate and other real and good faith controversies closely connected with them. These are the place of registration, real seat, administrative centre, business, control and any other criteria having a solid rational foundation in the relevant theory and practice of private international law and putting corporations and their actions under dominion of distinct legal systems.

As a result, depending on the place of forum, different states may extend their jurisdiction over corporate law issues arising between the parties on a cross-border basis. Thus the question once raised before a national court as to what nationality (allegiance) of a company registered in Poland, being run from Germany and acting in interests of English individuals living in Switzerland may become exceedingly vague and may give absolutely different answers, depending on the state of the forum where this question is raised.

This is due to specific legal theories advanced in all these civil and common law states[54] with respect to determination of *lex societatis* of the given corporation. For example, in Poland all and any issues on formation, merger, division, transformation or dissolution of moral persons (corporations) are submitted to the law of the country, in which this person is seated. That is the law of the state where this moral persons is established.[55]

With the help of these examples we may judge how difficult it is for law enforcers facing the problem of distinct treatment of personal law of corporations in distinct legal systems. As it may be seen all these legal theories underlying conflict of law rules set in national acts are a product of rationalization of the place and role of corporate law in national systems of law. And when dealing with legal issues closely connected with other states they rest on categories of private international law advanced in the relevant legal systems and exercising considerable influence upon proper operation and effect of national corporate law as to corporations as subjects of cross-border commercial and non-commercial transactions and individuals, being behind these corporations but owning and holding them.

The problem is that states agree that corporations should be submitted to one law. That is the personal law of corporations to be applied to the substance of cross-border corporate relations and other relations closely connected with them and to govern them. But in the age of freedom of

---

[54] Earlier I distinguished between two separate legal systems in the European Union: a system of civil law and a system of common law. They have always been considered as rival for the legal sources. But taking into view the modern trend, the line of separation becomes more and more invisible especially after the judgement in *Woodland v Swimming Teachers Association* [2012] UKSC 66; [2014] AC 537, in which at para 28 it is explicitly given that words used by judges are not to be treated as if they were the words of a statute.

[55] See Art. 17 of PAPIL 2011.

establishment in whichever state and jurisdiction individuals wish, to determine this law states prescribe differing propositions.

This may be law of the state in which:

(1) their registered offices (domicile)[56] are placed;

(2) their head offices are placed;

(3) the places of business are;

(4) control over these corporation is exercised.

Their effects vary along many lines in the resolution of legal problems arising in real and good faith controversies in foreign fora. We need to foresee all the negative legal consequences of actions when participating in a cross-border corporate activity or being closely connected with it.

The theory of incorporation seems preferable over other theories advanced in the private international law sphere in the appropriate formulas of *lex societatis* having distinct ends and consequently using different means to treat conflict of law problems in different states. This theory of incorporation is an exposition of the relevant policy of a sovereign state suggesting application of law of the place, where an association of individuals, furthering one common idea or specific end, is assumed in a separate legal quality. It means as a separate subject of law with its own distinct scope of rights and obligations separable from those, whose names are subscribed to a memorandum of a private law association or any other constitutional act prescribed by a national law of a corporation.

Linking nationality of a corporation with a state of incorporation precludes problems with its subjection to other states based on such ambiguous grounds as place of business and others and provides legal certainty in this particularly sensitive for states sphere of regulation of socio-economic relations.[57] Therefore, the main factor or criterion to determine corporate subjection should be that of the place of incorporation or registration as a company under the relevant companies act.

---

[56] See Art. 21 of the Swiss Federal Act on Private International Law, 1987, as amended until 1st July 2014 ("SFAPIL 1987"), where it is held that the registered office is deemed to be the domicile for the companies and trusts, created voluntarily as defined in the Hague Convention on the Law Applicable to Trusts and on their Recognition, 1985.

[57] Practically speaking, application of this formula is simple. The information on incorporation (name, address, legal form, persons managing a corporate activity etc.) is given in Articles of incorporation or association and confirmed by certificates of incorporation issued by competent public law authorities. These documents represent conclusive evidence of incorporation in strict accordance with requirements of corporate law of the chosen state and jurisdiction.

This autonomy of sovereign reasoning may not be destructed for the intrinsic attributes of states. These are supremacy and independence as per the form and substance of the sovereign activity of individuals comprising relevant states from the very formation of state organs to control over proper exercution of state functions by putting forward national customs and traditions within strictly limited boundaries of a definite territory. So the courts of one country cannot question the place of incorporation if that incorporation is recognised as legitimate in the host country.

This reasoning rests on the very idea of sovereignty, which is indestructible by itself. This means that:

(1) if there is a will or motivation of a people inhabiting a separate territory and acting as a sovereign assembly (or in other words – a state) to make any act, permission to go ahead with manifestation of this will out in the world will be given to those delegated with state functions;

(2) in all motivations and manifestations of the sovereign will states are free from any intrusions, instructions and recommendations from outside.

As a result, differences among states on forms of conflict of law regulation, being forms of the written sovereign reasoning, may never be challenged by another state. And this difference should be accepted as it is by theory and practice of conflict of law regulation in distinct sovereign states.

Among other questionable points of private international law of corporations is the problem of renvoi.[58] We know that conflict of laws is a collision or concurrence of laws in the governance of private law relations, when law enforcers are asked for the answer to the question, as to in accordance with which law they have to hear and determine private law cases with a foreign element brought in their hands. This problem is traditionally settled by conflict of law rules. They refer to appropriate material law rules of the chosen jurisdiction as a process universally adopted by states as the only way out of this problem despite the fact that this is lengthy.

---

[58] As a legal construction it may be expressed in this way in national private international law acts: *"If the foreign law specified as applicable by this Act specifies Polish law as governing the given relationship, then Polish law shall apply"* (see Art. 5 of PAPIL 2011. As it comes from the letter of this rule, Polish material law will apply to the substance and facts of all and any real and good faith controversies submitted to foreign law, which conflict of law issues do not consider as falling under the purview of a national system of law rather submit them to another system of law closely and substantially connected with them.

However, there is another way. It goes on further than the application of material law rules. It establishes the will of a foreign legislator, as to which law has to be applied in each specific case brought to court. It means that we do not solve a conflict of law problem, but make another one until the final settlement of the problem. However, this appears to be another conflict and another problem, having no connection with a private law dispute.

In the private international law sphere, dealing with legal rights and interests of those entering into private law transactions on a cross-border basis is a huge problem. A number of serious issues arise. What produces this juridical effect? Before answering this question we need to address other issues with which the first one is closely connected. Who decides what law to apply to private international law relations, which parties are in dispute? Based on what rules is this decision traditionally made? May this result be avoided by the parties?

When addressing these issues, first, it should be noted that law enforcers decide what law to apply to private international law relations brought to court using their own conflict of law rules *ex officio*. To make this decision they study private law disputes, think what law elements of private international law relations are closely connected and then apply material rules of the chosen law. This decision is made based on conflict of law rules of the place of the forum or rules explicitly designated by the parties when it is agreed with the objective (popular) will of a particular state closely connected with private international law relations. In the latter case the choice made by the parties precludes the very problem of going too far in conflict of law regulation. By the statute, agreement or in any other form prescribed by the law it submits private law relations to material law of the state found to be acceptable for the parties.

This juridical effect may be produced by deliberate actions of law enforcers, who in search of law applicable to private international law relations enter into details of the reasoning made by a foreign lawmaker in national rules of law over its own jurisdiction on these issues. The danger of going too far is much greater in that instance, when a choice of law is not limited by application of material law rules. For this reason attaching particular importance to a structure of conflict of law rules, nature and characteristics of judgments and commands made in them and addressed to law enforcers, there is no reason whatever to doubt as to the idea of law enforcement in such a case. It should end in the operation of material law rules after completion of a one-step act of the choice of applicable law in the process of settlement of conflicts of laws and interests of different states.

Evidence for this may be found in a number of legal acts addressing legal problems arising in the private international law sphere. They embody rules emanating from sovereign states to the effect not to *give permission* to a law enforcer to choose this or that law in a separate private law dispute, but *command them* to do so. And these commands should consistently be obeyed, even if there is no direct sanction to be imposed on a law enforcer for its non-fulfilment.[59]

The concept of renvoi cannot withstand a rigorous analysis. Hence, it will soon become apparent that it is premised on generating and protecting subjective will and interests within certain legal limits. To be specific – to give rise and protect private law rights and obligations of those already subjected to definite states and their laws and thus show interdependence of two sides of law.

These are legal rules (objective side) and legal relations (subjective side), which may never be considered separately. May any other law having no connection with these persons establish their rights and obligations or protect them without having any right to this? Or should not the court settle each specific dispute arising in private international law relations as they are found to be? Based on the given argumentation no other law may establish them and courts should resolve each particular private law case decisively one way or another taking into view the subjective will (consent) of its parties to leave their relations as they are.

There is no need to remind the reader that private international law is law rather than a mere technique. We may characterize this field of law as ordaining and practical law. If national law of corporations remains silent on private law issues of a particular action affecting the legal status or title to property and other rights on a cross-border basis, no other law may be operative instead. For this very reason in particular systems of law it is clearly stated that "…any reference to foreign law … must be considered as a reference to material and not conflicts law of the relevant state…".[60]

There is not much difficulty in discerning distinguishing marks of private international law of corporations as a separate legal institute of the relevant

---

[59] As an illustration read the following rule *"the judge shall apply the rules of the Turkish conflict of laws and the governing foreign law which is applicable in accordance with the said rules ex officio. If the provisions of the applicable foreign conflict of laws refer to another foreign law, this referral will only be taken into consideration in conflicts related to law of persons and property law. The substantive provisions of this foreign law thereof shall be applied"* (See Art. 2 of the TAPIPL 2007.

[60] See Art. 1260 of the Civil Code of Republic of Armenia, 1998, No. AL-239.

field of law. It is characterized by specific formal attributes, terminological apparatus and particular concepts underlying it.

3. SCOPE OF PRIVATE INTERNATIONAL LAW OF CORPORATIONS

This chapter examines the extent and subject matter of private international law of corporations and undertakes a detailed study of the guiding principles affecting the functioning of this legal institute in different systems of law. This study will start with the general object of law, which according to the proper signification of this term is a phenomenon of a specific rational activity based on certain supra-sensible *a priori* knowledge and taking the form of high moral principles of action.

The difference between natural law (traditionally said to be established by God) as invariable and eternal law and positive law (formulated and established by men), which as time passes undergoes immense material and immaterial changes through the relevant stages (development and growth or sometimes even stagnation and regress of law). Positive law when accompanied by sustainable growth becomes more and more complicated and ramified.

What else distinguishes natural law from positive law in a more clear manner for readers is that natural law provides for duties which have to be observed by all human beings regardless of age, race, gender, legal and financial status etc., while positive law – only those under an obligation of a specific law, and may be of a certain age, race, gender, legal and financial capacity and status etc. as the case may be but avoiding all forms of discrimination.

The operation of natural law is absolute, inviolable and indispensable notwithstanding time, place and circumstances for reasons given earlier, while the action of positive law is relative. It varies from imperative to optional or default rulings depending on a sphere of a socio-economic activity. And it is noteworthy that these rulings do not have force by themselves rather through operation of a specific lawmaking mechanism resting on supreme power of states and giving necessary impulse to the relevant rules of positive law.

Hence, based on provisions of natural law, all actions of human beings are viewed through the prism of their conformity to maxims of natural law, which ensure coexistence of all these human beings in the world formed by God for them. Whereas, based on rules of positive law, they are viewed through the prism of conformity or non-conformity to definite rules of law. These are both material and conflict of law rules, to which we referred earlier in the present paper as ensuring order and harmonious communication between all members of a community. Nevertheless, it should always be remembered that rules of law may never contradict or in any other way oppose to prescriptions of natural law on which they rest and which make communities grow and flourish.

We have demonstated the nature of private international law to be law derived from human will to govern private law relations burdened with a foreign element and determine a content of its separate legal institute resting on categories and notions elaborated by the theory of corporations with the help of the theory of legislation. These are cross-border corporate and other relations closely connected with them. Therefore, the content of private international law of corporations as a legal institute of the relevant field of positive law being under the purview of an objective (popular) will varies along a number of dimensions depending on the time, place and circumstances.

Thus far, the general object of positive law is to keep peace and facilitate normal communication inside a community. Whereas the main object of private international law of corporations is the ruling of cross-border corporate relations and other relations closely connected with them in order to ensure their sustainable development. Besides, when law is an expression of special force (not only coercive) to produce a predictable outcome for a community, private international law of corporations is a special force to preclude unpredictable rulings for public and private law interests of this cross-border activity.

As far as the theory of corporations is concerned, it has always been of a great importance for different states for a special idea of a corporation having different strictly functional characteristics allotted to it depending on the time, place and circumstances. It says that to become a subject of law this corporation needs to have a legal personality. That is the main category of the theory of corporations consisting in a peculiar legal state implying an aggregate of rights, obligations and responsibility as main attributes of a private law activity.

This means that the state of the place of incorporation decides whether to confer an association of persons with a separate legal personality necessary for participation in a private law activity or not. This state also decides on which terms to handle this particular issue. Hence, it is undeniable that this idea may never be harmonized for inherent essential points of difference in the interests and wills of those inhabiting states. The study of all these characteristics may take thousands of pages. Instead, I intend to show a clear correlation between this and other operative objective theories. These are the theory of certitude and the theory of will in private international law regulation of a corporate activity and other activity held by corporations.

Earlier, it was established that a corporation is the first and principal term, with which starts a system of notions of a legal institute of private international law of corporations. It is sufficiently recognized that this term is borrowed from corporate law. That is a field of law which produced a corporation as a separate, unique, strictly functional legal phenomenon recognized universally:

(1) partly through development of ideas inherent to Roman law, which legal principles continue to exist in all advanced legal systems;

(2) partly through successful operation of private international law rules.

These are the rules complying with a list of criteria: abstract, precise, non-discriminatory, and predictable for private and public law subjects.

The object of corporate law may be defined as that to govern actions of individuals in voluntary and functional associations they form pursuing one common legally enforceable idea or goal. Whereas the object of private international law of corporations is that to ensure non-discriminatory treatment of these actions on a cross-border basis through recognition of private international law rights and obligations. It is only for national law of a corporation to decide whether an association of individuals is a separate subject of law, which may freely enter into different types of a private law activity or not. This is clear enough.

What remains unclear is which corporate law issues are important for conflict of law regulation. Broadly speaking, we need to identify key issues which enable us to understanding the nature of cross-border corporate relations and other relations closely connected with them. However, we must remember that corporate law is law of shareholders, workers and executives aimed at bringing order into the activity undertaken by specific subjects produced by law, while private international law of corporations is concerned with a problem of the choice of law.

These are rules of substantive law applicable to a corporation as a subject of cross-border internal (labour, investment etc.) and external (purchase and sale of goods/services/technologies etc.) relations as the most important task of this legal institute. There are also other issues inextricably intertwined with the problem of the choice of rules applicable to the substance of all and any real and good faith controversies, which may arise or have already arisen between the parties of contractual and extra contractual relations in the corporate law sphere.

These are the choice of a forum and jurisdiction of courts to settle private international law disputes and enforce decisions made by foreign courts and consequently anchored in a foreign legal order. This jurisdiction is mainly determined based on nationality/domicile or habitual residence (for individual persons) or place of registered or head office, business, control (for corporations) of the defendant.[61]

Special prominence here is given to corporate law issues presenting a particular value for private international law of corporations. Among these issues we may distinguish:

- whether individuals are entitled to form a corporation in whichever state and jurisdiction they wish (save for the cases when they intend to evade laws of their home states)[62] and choose a form of a corporation they like;[63]
- whether a corporation is a distinct from the incorporators (and subject of law);[64]

---

[61] For the evidence see Italian legislation keeping that *"...la giurisdizione italiana sussiste quando il convenuto è domiciliato o residente in Italia..."*. That is the Art. 3 of Legge 31 maggio 1995, n. 218 (in Gazz. Uff., 3 giugno 1995, n. 128, s.o.) Riforma del sistema italiano di diritto internazionale private ("RSIDIP 1995") providing for the scope of Italian jurisdiction.

[62] With respect to this the most interesting and important point to be noted is that brought from the old practice of dealing with such issues. Thus, for example, when a corporation is formed in one state, and by express terms of its charter or another constitutional document it is created for doing business in another state, and business is done in that state, it must *"be assumed that the charter contract was made with reference to its laws, and the liabilities which those laws impose will attend the transaction of such business"* - *Pinney v.Nelson*, 22 Sup. Court Rep. (U.S.) 52 (1901).

[63] There is no doubt that the freedom of incorporation is one of the main socio-economic freedoms. It is set in numerous national and international legal acts to ensure private law rights and interests of investors in different socio-economic spheres of life of the relevant communities. These are communities that further the ideas of sanctity of labour and property, on which this freedom largely rests.

[64] The first principle of corporate law is that a corporation is a distinct subject of law. It is a form of a voluntary association of individuals characterized by limited liability and shared property, to which a home state concedes (and host states recognize) a separate legal capacity to exercise its free will over things and actions in order to make profit or attain any other legally enforceable common end (objective) under a separate name. It is distinct from those whose names are subscribed to a memorandum of a private law association or any other act prescribed by a national law of a corporation. Save for the breach of public interest through misuse, fraud, malfeasance or evasion of contractual or extra contractual obligations. In all cases attended with these circumstances corporate veil-piercing and other national law mechanisms to the same or common effect may be of

- whether a corporation is a distinct from a home state body (and subject of law);[65]
- what is a form of manifestation of rights conferred and obligations imposed by states to corporations;[66]
- to what a corporation may be entitled in its capacity of a subject of law;[67]
- whether there are attributes common to all corporations;[68]
- whether there is any reliable instrument to control the aim of a corporate activity and means employed by corporations to attain this aim.[69]

---

particular use by virtue of theories on fictitious corporations, theories on creation of false appearances or alike advanced in the relevant legal systems. Hence, it means that as soon it will be proved that a corporation has never been a distinct from the incorporators person, it will be considered as non-existent with all legal consequences of such non-existence for them.

[65] The second principle of corporate law is that corporations are private law subjects distinct from home states. Nevertheless, they are submitted to legally enforceable enactments of states on all issues of formation, reorganization, insolvency and termination. Besides these enactments govern all the issues pertaining to the legal capacity of corporations entering into any type of cross-border commercial and non-commercial relations.

[66] To exercise its free will over things and actions a voluntary association of individuals characterized by limited liability of shareholders and shared property needs to have a legal personality. That is the form of manifestation of distinct private law rights and obligations conferred (imposed) by a home state to this association to enter into distinct deals when pursuing the aim to make profit or attain any other legally enforceable common end (objective) inside a separate community or on a cross-border basis under a separate name.

[67] A corporation may participate in all types of a private law activity in accordance with its legally enforceable objective shown in a memorandum of association and other legal acts prescribed by national law as constitutional documents. In case of infringement of their private law rights and interests corporations may claim their protection in whichever legal order of the world in accordance with the relevant procedure. But there is commonly no defense to actions by corporations, which were set up in foreign states just to evade mandatory rules of states closely connected with relations they entered into to make profit. Even when nobody asks whether foreign corporations are carrying on business in their home states or not.

[68] Among main attributes common to all corporations we may distinguish 1) legal personality; 2) corporate property; 3) limited liability of incorporators; 4) separate system of governance and control. All these attributes play a prominent part in the model of corporations ensuring its proper functioning in whichever legal tradition.

[69] To guide the aim of a corporate activity and means employed by corporations to attain this aim is the main task of corporate law of the place of incorporation. From the very formation of a corporation this state controls legality of its activity held

We have now established the important corporate law issues for private international law of corporations. As the reader may observe these are issues, which refer to a sphere of the objective will demonstrating public opinion and prevail over the subjective will produced by the individual mind for the sensitivity of these issues for a home state of a corporation. And this delimitation of wills or interests is universally recognized and accepted.

Therefore there is no doubt that if answers to all these issues remain unaltered there is no need to revise existing conflict of law principles mostly employing ancient legal formulas and language and underlying this and other legal institutes of private international law as one of the essential forms, which this law takes. If this trend continues, we will have enduring and predictable conflict of law regulation in this sphere of a socio-economic activity.

Otherwise, certain conflict of law principles will have to be amended. But this will not happen soon, only after complete alteration of the national law framework resting on the idea of a national strictly functional association of individuals and generating appropriate corporate law forms and institutions having effect of form memory along different lines notwithstanding the time, place and circumstances. Hence, it means that nothing may affect a general idea, on which the theory of corporations rests.

In line with this we would like to consider a list of corporate law issues, which do not have any special bearing on conflict of law regulation:
- the legal form, character and particular end of corporations (save for the ones furthering illegal goals) are;
- whether there is a quantifiable number of types of corporations;
- whether there is one or a number of persons managing a corporation and many other aspects of a corporate activity.

Since these corporate law issues do not affect sovereign rights and interests of a home state or individual rights of persons inhabiting a state when viewed through the prism of private international law activity, ensured by conflict of law rules, taken to the heights of principles in national (autonomous) systems of law, they do not have any value in the private international law sphere.

When we speak of principles in the given context it is important to note that these are not general principles of material law rather principles formulated in corresponding forms of law to guide private law relations of corporations and other subjects of law bound by different systems of law in a way:

---

inside a separate community with the use of instruments specific for the relevant community.

(1) to protect private international law rights,

(2) to establish private international law obligations or sometimes

(3) to terminate them.

In the theory and practice of private international law regulation these principles are called as conflict of law principles.[70]

The are a limited number of these principles, unlike formulae required to adapt them in a specific manner in numerous forms of law enacted by sovereign states. They rest on a peculiar end of ruling consisting in the settlement of conflict of law problems. That is the ultimate obstacle to be removed for corporations waiting to expand profitable operations in foreign markets.

The main idea of conflict of law regulation consists in the properly made choice of material law as regards its subsequent application to private law relations with a foreign element. That is law closely connected with these private law relations through strong and permanent bonds of its subject or object with foreign public order or facts around these private law relations referring to foreign states. If a cause and effect approach is employed in conflict of law regulation, it will soon become apparent that its effect depends on the nature of the connection with a foreign state (cause). This has to be traced in each specific private international law case brought to court.

With respect to a subjective connection with a foreign state[71] it should be noted that all and any conflict of law problems should be resolved by appropriate means. We are speaking of conflict of law principles set in national law acts by those characterized by a specific nature and unique capacity conferred by states to determine, which material law rules to apply to foreign subjects of private law relations. Depending on the nature of these relations as well as a character of their ties with foreign states and their jurisdictions (nationality, residence etc.) these are:

(1) *lex societatis* referring to the personal law of corporations or

---

[70] It would be more accurate to call them principles resolving a problem of conflicting systems of law arising in private international law disputes brought to court. However, we will not insist on this for the reason that it has never been an easy task to define phenomena of private international law in a way acceptable for all and everybody.

[71] This subjective connection with a foreign state manifests itself in a foreign element (subject) in the structure of private international law relations. These are 1) a corporation (or corporations), 2) an individual (or a group of individuals) or even 3) a state entering into commercial and non-commercial relations with other subjects of law on a cross-border basis in a non-sovereign quality.

(2) *lex personalis* – to the national law of shareholders, employees.

In the age of the sanctity of individual rights conferred and protected by sovereign states these strong subjective bonds with a foreign state and jurisdiction may never be weakened.[72] But they should be distinguished from objective ones through presence of a foreign object in the structure of private international law relations (e.g. corporate property) tending to foreign law and jurisdiction. To resolve a dispute burdened with this element another conflict of law principle should be employed. That is *lex loci* as a conflict of law principle resting on the very idea of legal and technical mobility of labour and property when dealing with individual and real rights and obligations.

As far as legal facts closely connected with a foreign state and its jurisdiction are concerned[73] the same legal principles as are given above apply to private law cases burdened with them. It means that for the settlement of conflict of law problems we need to look more closely at the nature and character of legal bonds with a foreign state (or a number of states as the case may be). This is because all elements of private law relations which are mutually dependent are seated in definite public orders, by which they are bounded.

However, in some cases, there are issues which may be left unnoticed by law enforcers. If, for example, these are only the formal or casual bonds with a foreign state resting purely on contingent grounds, there will be a definite answer to the question, as to which precisely law has to be applied in each particular case brought to court. If, on the other hand, it is a permanent or logical connection free from any possible influences of contingent grounds we will have the answer we are searching for, guided by objective and just administration of law in this particular sphere of socio-economic relations.

Taking this as one of the key points of departure we may state that every structural element of private international law relations has its "seat" in a

---

[72] Thus, one could hardly deny that legal status of a national or foreign corporation entering into commercial and non-commercial relations across borders of one particular state should be governed by states based on legal principles (*lex societatis*) commonly formulated and established to ensure private law rights and interests of this corporation and all those being behind it (shareholders, employees etc.).

In this connection it is interesting to note that the term "national corporation" in the Bahamas embraces a company registered under the Companies Act, in which not less than 60% of its shares are beneficially owned by Bahamians (See Part 1 of Companies Act, 1992).

[73] These are, in particular, arrangement, amendment, implementation and termination of corporate, labour and investment contracts abroad.

definite system of law and jurisdiction. Depending on the type of private law relations this "seat" of a structural element may be extremely important as to the effect of conflict of law regulation of private law disputes brought to court, whether they are submitted to one state or another.

Considering the practical nature of private international law of corporations, the choice of private law instrument to resolve conflicts of corporate laws of different sovereign states may be explained only empirically. It depends on a great variety of circumstances in particular cases making up even a chain of circumstances around a specific private law case placed in the hands of the court to resolve. That is the one resting on a specific practice of reconciliation of conflicting public law interests of sovereign states in a private law sphere.

The private international law practice has long elaborated a number of means to settle these conflicts in a manner meeting both public and private law interests. These are conflict of law rules taken by the theory to the heights of principles for their specific role in resolution of peculiar legal problems, which judges and other persons charged with them face in the corporate law sphere. Each conflict of law rule is a separate legal approach. It has long been developed but has not lost its particular practical value for its capacity to materially affect private law cases, in particular, rights of those entering into private international law relations.

The number of these principles is strictly limited, unlike material law principles. They rest on the idea that every person and thing in this material world belong to a definite place. As a consequence only the law and jurisdiction in this peculiar place may have effect in cross-border corporate and other disputes closely connected with them. When arranging these rules into separate groups in accordance with observed similarities, there is no absolute criterion for the complete and all-inclusive classification, except when it is undertaken for a very limited goal.

The most important principles relevant to this publication are:

- on the nature of corporate obligations and other obligations closely connected with them we may distinguish two main types of conflict of law rules. These are rules the application of which rests on the idea of liberty to govern contractual obligations (e.g. *lex voluntatis, lex loci actus* etc.) and rules premised on the idea of legal paternalism as well as other operative ideas to deal with extra contractual relations of the parties (e.g. *lex personalis, lex loci delicti commissi* etc.);
- on the nature of a foreign element (a foreign subject or a foreign object) in the structure of corporate law relations, conflict of law rules fall into two

types: those relating to persons (e.g. *lex societatis, lex personalis*) and things (e.g. *lex voluntatis, lex loci* etc.);
– on the end of regulation, all conflict of law rules fall into those ensuring public interests of a home state and its nationals (*lex societatis, lex personalis*) or private interests of immediate parties of legal relations burdened with a foreign element (*lex voluntatis, lex loci actus* etc.).

Having finished with this short classification of conflict of law rules in the corporate law sphere, which are always public and intermediary (so called "rules for courts") it is time to look more closely at these principles constituting the essence of this particular legal institute. We will scrutinize the main principles attributable to the ruling of cross-border corporate, labour, investment and other commercial and non-commercial relations in a corporate law sphere, from which much substance of this private international law institute may be observed.

These are conflict of law principles of *lex societatis, lex personalis, lex loci* and *lex voluntatis* employed by private international law of corporations to resolve all and any conflicts of states in a corporate law sphere. The issues which may be governed by these private international law rules differ in each case brought to court.

The first tier of these issues relates to formation, reorganization, insolvency and termination of corporations as relevant subjects of law (including private international law). The second tier of these issues is concerned with legal status of corporations as subjects of private international law relations. In the most comprehensive generalization that is the scope of rights, obligations and responsibility of a corporation as a subject of private law when it is considered both in statics and dynamics. The third tier of issues relates to a cross-border commercial and non-commercial activity of corporations as a main trend of this age.

This gives us enough reasons to characterize private international law of corporations:
– **on the subject matter of regulation** – as a body of firmly set directly applicable rules, conflict of law rules and international jurisdiction rules governing cross-border corporate relations and other relations closely connected with them in a manner predictable for a home state, incorporators, employees and other persons involved;
– **on the method of regulation** – as a body of rules governing these relations based primarily on commands (mandatory regulation) ensuring public law interests of the relevant communities;
– **on the purpose** – as a body of rules (directly applicable rules, conflict of law rules and international jurisdiction rules) addressing complicated

legal and jurisdictional issues pertaining to the choice of law and forum to be made in a corporate law sphere in a way preventing public interests of the appropriate states from being impaired.

3.1. Particulars of the use of *lex personalis*

When examining the details of conflict of law regulations in this context "the whole of the law which we observe relates either to persons, or to things, or to actions". So, it is the right time to "speak of persons: for it is useless to know the law without knowing the persons for whose sake it was established".[74]

Citizens and non-citizens (foreigners, strangers) require their legal rights and interests to be duly ascertained, established, recognized and protected on a cross-border basis. These are legal rights and interests of those who live abroad or enter into cross-border commercial and non-commercial deals singly or jointly with others.

Taking this as the main point of our departure we would like to start this section with the following observation. For centuries the only conflict of law principle commonly employed by sovereign states to ensure individuals with all privileges of ex-territoriality has been *lex personalis*. It is the oldest private international law principle in the relevant systems of law constructed by sovereign states with the aim of settling the endless diversity of conflicts of personal, real and mixed statutes arising in a private international law sphere.

The main idea of this conflict of law principle consists in the reference to the personal law (in French - *statut personel de l'étranger*) to determine civil status and legal capacity of foreigners, when they enter into private international law disputes characterized by a specific goal, means and consequences assigning a special character to them.[75] These are disputes resulting from private law relations, in which structure all elements constitute an object of separate study and research. These elements are "seated" in different systems of law and pertain to distinct structural elements of the given systems.

This principle expresses the idea of supremacy of law (be it national or foreign law) giving rise to rights and obligations of individuals to enter into

---

[74] J.B. Moyle trans. 1911. "Justinian, Institutes," Oxford.

[75] Under the term *"personal law of individuals"* we mean law of the place of their nationality and governing their civil status and capacity as well as a scope of family rights and duties. With respect to individuals without nationality or with indeterminate nationality the law of the place of domicile or habitual residence shall be deemed to be a personal law.

civil or commercial law relations singly or jointly with others. Hence, it means that this principle holds individuals in the centre of all valuations and thus affects:

(1) their status and capacity;
(2) nature and state of property;
(3) nature, scope and effect of contractual and extra contractual obligations through strong and stable ties with one particular state conferring these individuals with a mixture of civil rights, duties and responsibility.

Having thus ascertained the main idea of *lex personalis* we may say that none of the other conflict of law principles of conflict of law regulation of civil law relations with a foreign element (in particular, e.g. *lex societatis, lex loci, lex voluntatis*) may be considered in this way. What is also distinguishable in this connection is that practical significance and scientific exposition *de la loi personnelle étrangère* (in French) have never varied regardless of the time, place and circumstances.

It deals with a scope of legal capacity of individuals entering into private international law relations in a manner suggesting common satisfaction with effect of the conflict of law regulation. This is mainly because this conflict of law principle stands in the position of power or dominion of individuals over things they own and actions they make guided by their free will within definite limits set by states to ensure freedom of other individuals. These are the limits of good faith conduct and are in accordance with main postulates of natural law.[76]

In the private law sphere this power or dominion is enveloped into legal categories of rights and interests, to which much theoretical and practical significance has always been attached. In line with obligations, these are key categories of the theory of law as the main instrument to develop a legal thought (which is by itself a strictly autonomous development) in the right direction to ensure interests of freedom, when both rights and obligations tend to limit the originally unlimited nature of the subjective will. With reference to this, freedom is natural and inalienable right and reflected in this way in legal acts made by sovereign states. Without it we would never have numerous legal orders generating public and private law rights and obligations, which are initially rooted as well as nurtured and inspired by

---

[76] The notion of good faith conduct typically used as a yardstick to distinguish between proper and improper conduct was at first only instinctive, but with the passage of time it became consciously developed in legal theory and practice and thus set in national legislation of all advanced jurisdictions.

this unique legal phenomenon, to which special attention has always been paid by all those charged with law making and law enforcing functions.

As to a specific form of its expression (subjective will), in order to be duly expressed in rightful thoughts and actions and when necessary to be protected it should be supported by the objective will. That is, law as a very powerful instrument in the hands of sovereign states determining what constitutes rights and abuse of rights as two opposite but closely connected categories of law, which may never be viewed separately.

They are employed to reach two main aims:

(1) to ensure the freedom in a cooperative community because rights may never be considered otherwise than a symbol for what is just, free as well as of equal nature, opportunity and value for all and everybody; and

(2) to prevent a collision of subjective wills, which may only be met by their guidance in the right direction.

That is the direction which makes a community composed of persons from different social groups grow and prosper in the long run.

To handle these issues legislators incorporate into a national legal system the term "good faith" as an extremely valuable substantive device employed both by legal theory and practice on a wide range of private law issues and distinguishing between legal (good faith) and illegal (bad faith) conduct in different spheres of a socio-economic activity.

In the private international law sphere this freedom rests on the very idea of subjection of each person to a definite legal order ensuring proper execution of rights and obligations within a separate community and even outside it. This subjection is premised on the idea of nationality or in the absence of nationality on the domicile (or permanent residence) of a person having a particular juridical effect on the settlement of a conflict of law dispute.[77] This idea manifests itself in a close and permanent connection of a person with a certain state in the broad signification of this term embracing its law, language, cultural, religious and other customs and traditions extending their force over a definite sovereign territory.

---

[77] For instance, under Art. 3 of PAPIL 2011 "...*where the statutory law provides that the national law shall be governing but the citizenship of a given person cannot be established or a person does not have citizenship of any state or the substance of the national law cannot be established, the law of the state in which their place of residence is situated shall apply; if there is no place of residence, the law of the state in which the place of their ordinary stay is situated shall apply*".

So, from birth, a person (and in particular cases even earlier) their rights and legal interests are duly protected by a sovereign state and they themselves become an integral part of a definite community developing its unique spirit, interests and values. Paying special attention to the specific nature of rights and legal capacity of individuals deriving from home states and having no analogies in the private international law sphere, how is this law applicable to foreigners entering into cross-border civil law relations? Distinct answers should be given to the following issues: What is this law and how is it determined? What are these rights and how do they arise?

When viewed from the position of positive law, which must suffice in the present context, that is the law of a sovereign state with which this foreigner is closely connected through bonds of nationality, domicile or permanent residence (a home state). Home states not only confer and protect individual rights, which are termed "positive". They also ensure formal expression of these rights in territorial legal acts and their development for the subsequent recognition on a cross-border basis in their original scope or with some limitations set by host states.

This scope of recognized rights depends on a legal regime set by a host statewith regard to foreigners. First, we are speaking of the following fundamental individual rights, which are kept by the constitution and other national law acts as supported by rights of action to be used until their extinction. They are identical or similar and consist in:

(1) freedom of association;

(2) freedom of movement;

(3) liberty;

(4) freedom of thought;

(5) self-determination;

(6) due process of law to be kept by individuals.

Another issue arises as to what may hinder enjoyment of these rights on a cross-border basis, when several distinct states come into contact? The point is that these rights have always been associated with a dignity of independence resting on a specific social nature and constitution of individuals. Their non-recognition may hinder their enjoyment outside the borders of a home state. It may happen when a host state has no intention to recognize the sovereignty of a separate community and legality of relevant acts or in many other cases of cynical disregard of sovereign rights of other states over a good number of legal issues burdened with foreign elements. As a result this triggers retortions, which have inevitably been regarded as legitimate actions from home states from the standpoint of international law.

This cannot happen in the system of law where conflict of law rules explicitly emphasize that the legal status of foreigners entering into private law relations in a host state should be governed by their national law (in French - *par la loi de son domicile*) thus excluding application of any other law.

Staying with the particulars of *lex personalis* use in the private international law sphere to the extent, which this issue requires, when this sphere is viewed in an active context, through the prism of private international law relations, we need not answer the question where these private international law relations arise. It also makes no sense to know where they will be completed for a close connection of these legal relations with one law and one jurisdiction[78] on a specific list of issues dealing with:

- legal status of individuals (its limits in commercial and non-commercial spheres);
- capacity of volition and action (who may not have this capacity), other terms to acquire private law rights and obligations in commercial and non-commercial spheres;
- origination, validity, execution and termination of marital and parental rights, rights of children, rights of inheritance and other rights, which come under this category (family rights).

These are issues under the purview of civil law, the source of law for all other fields in a private law sphere, in particular:

(1) corporate law shaping specific forms of the joint activity of individuals in different spheres of the socio-economic life of the relevant community;

(2) commercial law as the law building up a separate type of activity aimed at making a profit;

(3) labour law guiding all forms of employment as well as rights, obligations and responsibility of the immediate parties of employment relations enveloped into a particular legal form etc.

In their classical form we know them starting from the sixteenth or nineteenth century (depending on the field of law).[79] For the particular role of these issues in sustainable socio-economic growth of separate communities will be carefully studied later in the book.

---

[78] These are the law and jurisdiction of the state with which individuals are closely connected. This makes only one conflict of law principle be put forward. It is *lex personalis* perfectly serving both public and private law interests when ensuring the unity of legal status of individuals for the purpose of conflict of law regulation.

[79] By way of illustration in England incorporation of commercial law into the relevant system of common law dates back to the second half of the eighteenth century.

There has always been a peculiar connection between commercial, corporate, labour and civil law dealing with private law relations into which individuals enter based on different reasons affecting their legal status. These reasons demarcate these separate branches of law characterized by a particular subject matter and methodology resulting in distinct guiding principles.

The ruling of different types of legal relations submitted to them, these principles may never be compatible without impairing substantial public and private law interests. Even in the sphere of private international law regulation these private law relations are treated differently based on distinct legal reasoning underlying them. As a result cross-border commercial and labour relations are guided by *lex loci* and *lex voluntatis*, when relevant. Corporate law deals are governed by *lex societatis* and civil law deals by *lex personalis*.

All these issues relating to legal status, capacity of volition and execution of individual rights depend on the personal statute of an individual entering into cross-border private law relations to attain one specific end in commercial or non-commercial spheres.

There are no exceptions. This means that in each specific case brought to court for the settlement of a private international law dispute the law enforcer will look to the national law of a foreign individual to answer the question whether this person is legally capable of entering into cross-border commercial and non-commercial deals or not. A positive answer to this private law issue will be given then and only then, when all requirements of the personal statute of this foreign individual are properly met.

Otherwise this person may not enter into any deals except when a host state may remedy this lack of legal capacity under the personal statute of a foreign individual and thus remove obstacles to validity of commercial and non-commercial deals into which this foreign individual enters on a cross-border basis.[80] In that instance, competing interests of freedom of contract prevail over other interests, be them interests of the weak party advanced by the theory of legal paternalism or any other interests.

---

[80] As an illustration see the rules of the Turkish law which state that *"legal capacity of a person shall be governed by his/her national law. A person lacking legal capacity pursuant to his/her national law shall be bound by the transaction he/she has concluded if he/she is legally capable under the law of the state where he/she has concluded the transaction. Transactions pertaining to family law and inheritance law as well as"in rem" rights on immovable property located in foreign countries are excluded from the scope of this provision"* (Art. 9 of the TAPIPL 2007).

By virtue of the theory of legal paternalism resting on equity in private law relations this conflict of law principle applies to all cases of business-to-consumer contracts with crushingly vague obligations on the side of business, when non-commercial or non-professional interests of consumers are wholly submitted to commercial and professional interests of the business.

A home state cannot remain silent in case of business-to-consumer contracts drafted in a way to discriminate, when consumers are considered as a means to attain a specific end of business rather an equal party having definite legal interests, rights and privileges. In order to render them equitable and transform compulsion into mutuality required in this sphere lawmakers extend strict limits of public and private law rights and set appropriate obligations.

In the present context, it should be observed, the general theory of law mainly views individuals from their capacity or incapacity to share private law rights and obligations[81] with others. For this very reason it makes use of the following terms "subject of law" and "subject of private law relations" to those who may have capacity of volition and may direct their will to a specific end.

However, the core of the theory of legal paternalism in conflict of law regulation of cross-border business-to-consumer contracts is the idea of protecting those, who may acquire rights or incur civil law obligations to maintain their commitments. But these obligations are gross or means by which they should be discharged are unacceptable. This idea places civil rights of individuals under special protection triggering a corresponding mechanism in conflict of law regulation to exempt serious negative consequences for them.[82]

---

[81] Rights and obligations are two closely connected categories, which may not exist one apart from the other. In the theory of law these are two elements of legal status of the subject of law.

[82] Thus, when considering distance contracts, "...*when the parties have determined that the contract shall be governed by the law of a State which is not a member of the European Community, a judge before whom that law is invoked is required to disregard it and apply the more protective provisions of the law applicable at the consumer's normal place of residence deriving from transposition of Directive 97/7/EC of the European Parliament and Council dated 20 May 1997 concerning consumer protection in regard to distance contracts, and Directive 2002/65/EC of the European Parliament and Council dated 23 September 2002 concerning distance marketing of financial services to consumers, when the contract has a close link with the territory of one or more European Community Member States; this condition is deemed to have been met if the consumers are resident in a Member*

It is evident, therefore, that by the use of *lex personalis* the national state of an individual plays an active role in conflict of law regulation and supplements what is inadequate in cross-border business-to-consumer contracts to avert risks of further losses for nationals.

In cases of this kind a court is a specific instrument in the hands of states striking the balance between distinct legal theories (freedom of contract and legal paternalism) in the private international law sphere and restoring competing rights and interests of those entering into this specific type of contracts. For example, this law provides for the cases when terms of business-to-consumer contracts become non-binding for consumers or when the seller's liability arising under such contracts may neither be excluded nor restricted if the seller plans to evade strict rules of law by other practices.

By virtue of directly applicable national law rules precluding conflict of law problems business-to-consumer contracts may be viewed as null and void with effect of this nullity and voidance for individuals aggrieved by the aggressive commercial practice.[83] That is the practice aimed at limiting the freedom of choice by distorting the consent of consumers or impeding the exercising of their contractual rights.

As to directly applicable rules, these are material law rules of the state of a forum or some other state recognized as rules of the state closely and substantially connected with private international law relations. Their application cannot be precluded by any other rules explicitly designated by the parties or provided otherwise for the public interest contained in the nature, aim, substance and effect of these rules having a particular effect for the enacting state.

National law rules with the same effect provide for the terms causing a significant imbalance in the parties' rights and obligations under consumer contracts contrary to the requirement of good faith and to the detriment of a consumer (unfair terms). In order to consider these terms as unfair and consequently non-binding for the consumer one should look at the nature of a business-to-consumer contract and circumstances that surrounded their

---

State" (See Art. L121-20-15 of French Consumer Code. Last amendment translated : Order No. 2005-1086 of 1 September 2005).

[83] *"Le contrat conclu à la suite d'une pratique commerciale agressive mentionnée aux articles L. 121-6 et L. 121-7 est nul et de nul effet"* (See Art. L132-10 of French Consumer Code. Last amended on 11 march 2017).

making. It is also worth uncovering the true intention of the parties at this as well as the assumed effect of their execution.[84]

From what has been given above it is evident that *lex personalis* is the main conflict of law principle in the relevant system of principles introducing us into a distinct field of law, which is private international law. This conflict of law principle settles legal problems arising in private international law disputes, in which nationality (domicile or residence as the case may be) of the parties involved makes a particular sense over any other place and other connection with another legal order.

However, there are private law cases in which reference to a personal law of individuals may result in infringement of public interests of states closely connected with private law relations with a foreign element. These are cross-border corporate relations and other relations closely connected with them requiring specifically formulated conflict of law rules resting on the idea of nationality, domicile or residence of well-organized groups of individuals to ensure unity and integrity of corporations in all issues relevant to formation, activity, reorganization, insolvency and termination tending to two or more distinct sovereign states for the further treatment based on special material law acts.

3.2. Particulars of the use of *lex societatis*

Difficulties in the private law sphere have for a long time been closely connected with the peculiar nature and specific legal status of corporations as subjects of law. The main cause is the purely legal nature and state of corporations appearing to be the product of the objective will of a people inhabiting a distinct territory thus recalling to everybody the very same idea.

---

[84] And if we just have a short look at the national legislation we will find a long indicative and non-exhaustive list of terms, among which may be found as follows:

– *A term which has the object or effect of excluding or limiting the trader's liability in the event of the death of or personal injury to the consumer resulting from an act or omission of the trader. This does not include a term which is of no effect by virtue of section 65 (exclusion for negligence liability).*

– *A term which has the object or effect of inappropriately excluding or limiting the legal rights of the consumer in relation to the trader or another party in the event of total or partial non-performance or inadequate performance by the trader of any of the contractual obligations, including the option of offsetting a debt owed to the trader against any claim which the consumer may have against the trader.*

– *A term which has the object or effect of making an agreement binding on the consumer in a case where the provision of services by the trader is subject to a condition whose realisation depends on the trader's will alone"* (See Schedule 2, Part 1 "List of terms" of the Consumer Rights Act 2015).

These are sovereign states that confer associations of individuals with distinct legal rights and duties deriving from them as well as rights and duties initially inherent to individuals (incorporators) but separable from all of them.

In the private international law sphere this distinction of private law rights and duties results in peculiar regulation resting on their submission to the law and jurisdiction of the place of a corporate nationality or domicile.[85] This peculiar nature and specific legal status of corporations would never enable it to meet the pressing economic, political and social concerns of the time and place without continual changes to corporate law in each specific state adapting to their local circumstances.

Each corporation should complete its own particular goal in internal and external relations for which its setting up was sanctioned by competent authorities of a home state. However, these are not revolutionary changes, which are unacceptable in the sphere of ruling of private law relations which are sensitive for communities. Instead, it is sustainable growth of corporate law to refine the legal model of corporations shaping the relevant theory to meet pressing needs of a definite community.

Turning to conflict of law regulation of corporate and other relations closely connected with them it is worth mentioning that gives rise to corporate law rights. We know what these rights are and by what means they are determined. However, someone may always say that they have trouble answering the question as to which state may establish these rights when exercised on the basis spanning many states and their jurisdictions.

In these cases the idea of inalienable rights of nationality should be put forward: it is impossible even for common theoretical purposes, for a corporation to be a subject of private law on something different from a home state with which it is inextricably linked from foundation until termination or change of corporate seat requiring completion of all the necessary corporate law procedures.[86] Only a home state decides, whether to cover an association of individuals acting jointly in pursuance of one

---

[85] It differs from those of members of corporate/non-corporate persons, whose names are subscribed to memoranda of private law associations or any other acts prescribed by governing law as constitutional acts.

[86] For a more objective view see Art. 19 of the PAPIL 2011 "...*after the seat of the moral person has been moved to another country, the moral person shall be subject to the law of this country since the moment of the transmission. Legal personality obtained under the law of the previous seat shall be maintained, if it is provided by the law of each of the countries concerned. Transmission of the seat within the European Economic Area shall never lead to loss of moral personality...*".

common idea in a specific legal capacity or not and what rights to confer to this association of individuals.

In theory and practice of private international law this phenomenon is termed a "national law of a corporation" or its *lex originis*. This means the law of a state conferring a corporation with rights and obligations and taking control over this corporation in its activity outside its territorial borders. However different are the theories of corporations advanced in distinct sovereign states assuming a peculiar role of corporations in sustainable growth of national economies, they all agree in the necessity to apply common legal approaches, when determining and recognizing the scope of rights and obligations of corporations in the private international law sphere.

Expressed in conflict of law principles these approaches apply to a multiplicity of private law cases. This is understood as the only way out of problems concerned with what law to apply to a corporation as the main subject of a private law activity closely connected with two or more states.[87]

It thus appears that *lex societatis* is a rule on subjection of a corporation in its cross-border activity to a home state reduced to a simple general principle addressing a broad range of private law issues given in slightly different wording in numerous national law acts around the world:

- formation of a corporation:
    (1) method of forming;
    (2) name, address, legal form, structure and composition, including all alterations and their legal effect;
    (3) shares (nature, value, numbering, transferability) and share capital of a corporation (terms of alteration);
    (4) legal status of a corporation (scope of its rights, duties and responsibility);
    (5) limitations (constitutional and others) which do not affect its legal status etc.;

---

[87] Thus, for example, on account of the origin of corporate nationality seated in a home state, if a German corporation carries on a trade activity in the UK, the Companies Act of England and Wales cannot define its legal status as a subject of private international law relations because it is a foreign national in the UK. In this connection it is worth citing provisions of the Bill S. 1876, introduced in the Senate of the United States on 14 May 1971 by Mr Burdick "*...for the purposes of this section and section 1302 of this title: a corporation shall be deemed a citizen of every State and foreign state by which it has been incorporated and of the State or foreign state where it has its principal place of business*".

- shareholders participation:
    (1) rights, privileges (title to a portion of funds, right to participate in profit, right to vote, information right etc.) and duties of shareholders; transactions requiring their approval (substantial property transactions and others);
    (2) claims and proceedings by members (as to calling meetings, circulation of statements, independent reports on the activity of corporations etc.);
    (3) registration of new shareholders (terms and requirements);
    (4) responsibility of shareholders with respect to all and any debts of corporations;
- representation of a corporation:
    (1) requirements to the number of persons and persons themselves dealing with governance of corporations (requirements to the minimum and maximum age, nationality etc.);
    (2) appointment and removal of these persons;
    (3) powers delegated to these persons;
    (4) validity of their acts;
    (5) legal effect of the breach by these persons of governing law, articles of association or statutes;
- reorganization of a corporation as a means to alter its legal status:
    (1) method;
    (2) requirements to different types of legal forms, procedure and legal effect;
- insolvency and termination of a corporation: method, terms, requirements and legal effect.[88]

---

[88] In this connection, the corporate contract cannot be submitted to any other law than national law of a corporation for the following reasons:

– that is a separate type of contracts by which individuals and other subjects of law contract peculiar legal status, the one of the separate subject of law, which is law of the state of incorporation;

– that is the form of the joint activity of individuals and other subjects of law pursuing common economic (financial) interest in a way to prevent public interests of the home state from being infringed.

– that is the only form accompanying the above-mentioned joint activity of individuals and other subjects of law until its very cessation.

Hence, it means that in the corporate law sphere nothing done or concluded by the parties to a corporate contract may legally bind them and third parties without state authorization. For this reason all issues of the form, essential terms as well as arrangement, execution, alteration and completion, a corporate contract as a separate type of private law agreements shall be exclusively governed by national

All these issues will have a legal (juridical) effect for incorporators and third parties only if they are settled in strict accordance with a personal law of corporations. That is the law of a state fixing upon an association of individuals by their consent a status of a distinct subject of law and extending a legal effect of this fixing on other states through the relevant instruments of recognition of such rights and duties by foreign states.

This exclusive authoritativeness of *lex societatis* is accepted by all jurists and practitioners of law around the world split into different territorial systems of law, serving as a point of departure for the structuring of a great number of distinct legal acts and facts consistent with public policy, public security and public health of the relevant communities.

Thus, by way of illustration, representative authority as a specific phenomenon of corporate law with the view to a particular nature of relations arising between corporations and their representatives and suggesting their special treatment, is governed by *lex societatis* of a corporation. This means that the legal capacity of a director acting on behalf of and in the interests of a certain corporation at arrangement, execution, alteration and completion of a share-purchase agreement, merger agreement or any other deal with a foreign company over shares in its capital will depend on the national law of a corporation. This law, which is also the law of the place where this representative authority is practised or law of the representative's work place will set sufficiently clear and precise conditions, which a director should thoroughly comply with in order to place a particular corporation under a commitment against all and any third parties.

Nevertheless, all and any issues pertaining to the form, substance, validity and legal effect this particular deal will be governed by *lex societatis* of a foreign company. That is the case when the form cannot be separated from the content. The evidence for this is found in the directly applicable rules in national private international law acts. For example, in Switzerland it is

---

law of a corporation as law, giving rise to a separate subject of law. Because this contract is only a step in the process of setting up a corporation. And as a rule the unity of the whole process should be respected.

In a broad sense of this term "national law of a corporation" embraces, in addition to corporate law rules 1) civil law rules governing general issues of arrangement, amendment and termination of corporate law relations, 2) corporate law rules governing specific issues on this type of contracts and a peculiar type of private law rights, to which it gives rise and 3) rules of any other field of law (banking, commercial etc.) governing peculiar issues on a specific type of the chosen corporate law form for a joint commercial and non-commercial activity in common financial (economic) interest.

stated that "...the merger agreement must comply with the mandatory company law provisions of the laws governing the involved companies, including the provisions concerning form".[89]

It thus appears that the greatest significance and scope is given to this conflict of law principle dealing with essential issues of law of corporations with cross-border impact and ensuring its unity. That is the unity in all corporate actions affecting legal status of corporations and complementing each other. This principle suffers no exceptions as to settlement of a long list of complicated issues equally affecting a corporation and individuals, who hold it for some personal economic (financial) interests. Currently that is the privilege of an exterritorial activity and control in different socio-economic spheres once granted by states to individuals and leaving open new opportunities to them.

The law of corporate nationality of the party effecting characteristic performance under business-to-business transactions caused by some professional or commercial aim will govern them in the absence of express or implied choice of applicable law, when a judge is searching for the law closely or substantially connected with private law relations. To respond to this test of the close or substantial connection, a judge studies the nature and character of the private law relations in dispute to answer the question as to which party renders it effective under a specific head.

The law applicable in all EU Member States is:
(1) seller under the contract for the sale of goods;
(2) service provider under the contract for the provision of services;
(3) franchisee under a franchise contract etc.[90]

In this case a judge will be guided by a conflict of law rule *lex societatis* of its own legal system in order to choose material law rules based on the relevant determining provisions to govern specific private international law relations brought to court.

Had it not been *lex societatis*, a conflict of law principle governing a broad list of corporate law issues closely connected with two or more states, numerous other legal principles would never have furnished solution of legal problems in a way it is expected and desired in this separate private law sphere. This is particularly important at the extended composition of corporations premised on foreign direct and indirect investments as well as their

---

[89] See Art. 163c of the SFAPIL 1987.
[90] See Art. 4 of the Regulation of the European Parliament and of the Council on the law applicable to contractual obligations (Rome I), 2008, No 593/2008.

extended functionality through rendering services and making works abroad, when it results in a conflict of personal and real statutes distinctly affecting private law rights and obligations.

But this should not be the case. As ever, corporate law relations in their whole complexity and diversity are governed solely by national corporate law, the same is true for cross-border corporate relations and other relations closely connected with them which are also guided by national law of corporations. This all maintains the stable and unchallengeable position of *lex societatis* in well-organized national systems of conflict of law principles as essential principles of regulation of private international law relations on the formation, composition, representation, reorganization, insolvency and termination of corporations. Assessing the direct bearing of this conflict of law principle on these relations, that is the main legal principle leading us into a separate legal institute (private international law of corporations) dealing with cross-border corporate relations and other relations closely connected with them in the system of the relevant field of law (private international law).

Since the time when this conflict of law principle was brought forth and received its juridical basis in the relevant form *lex societatis* was considerably developed by jurists and practitioners of law. Through their vigorous and determined attempts it was recognized as one of the main legal principles guiding jurists and other persons charged with settlement of private international law problems in the right direction and results infallibly in the choice of applicable law and jurisdiction predictable for the parties of cross-border legal relations.

The reason for steady and harmonious framing and development of this conflict of law principle rests on the firm basis. These are ideas of:
- a state as a form of initially strictly functional association of individuals bound together by common cultural, religious, geographical and other customs and traditions and characterized by the sovereignty in internal relations and equality in external (international law) relations;
- law as a purely national development having two mutually dependent and mutually supplanting sides. These are legal rules and legal relations proceeding upon objective and subjective will and interests;
- private law rights conferred by a state to an association of individuals by operation of law and characterized by a close, continuous and indissoluble connection with a home state, which may never be severed completely.

The nature of the end pursued when applying this conflict of law principle is unchanged. From the start it deals with a problem of the choice of governing law based on a specific purely practical method as a proper means to realize this end. Its use makes law enforcers reconcile conflicting interests of states in a peculiar way. It treats law as a duty when all and any acts contrary to rules containing public interest and public policy in the national legislation are null and void by the very operation of law. Law may be used as a right, and this is important in the private law sphere. There is a sphere of the parties' volition as to which law has to be applied to specific private cases burdened with one or more foreign elements tending to separate public orders.

This conflict of law principle is founded upon the idea of a corporation, which is nevertheless not uniform. We refer to this idea as a generalized expression of what a corporation ought to be rather it is in specific circumstances of the place and time. This idea is the most comprehensive generalization made within a definite state based on a specific practice taking distinct forms. Hence, it means that if these national ideas of corporations do not oppose to each other, they do differ depending on the place where they are advanced and circumstances around these ideas, which nevertheless do not affect the substance of conflict of law regulation. It rests on the very same principles adopted by states, and on close and continuous legal bonds of a corporation with a home state, its system of law and courts.

In this connection another issue arises as to whether something may lessen these close and continuous legal bonds of a corporation with a national state and jurisdiction? Endowed with a legal capacity throughout its existence a corporation is subject to a home state in its cross-border commercial and non-commercial activity. Hence, in all issues relevant to its activity a corporation is guided by the law of a home state in specific ways.

Nevertheless, formulae of the given private international law principles may take different forms resting on legal theories of the real seat, administrative centre, control etc., referring to different states and jurisdictions and expressing mutual relationship between states and persons.[91] They are irrelevant to corporate law forms because do not directly deal with corporate law relations rather conflicting interests of states in this particularly important sphere. But this difference in approaches applicable to determination of the national law of a corporation is absolutely fundamental. Such a state of affairs demonstrates how distinct are public interests of sovereign states in this sphere of conflict of law regulation.

There is another issue closely connected with this, as to whether a corporation may have double or multiple nationality. Corporations are a

---

[91] For details see paragraph **2.4**.

product of law. That is the law through which enactment this corporation is given distinct rights and duties in both private and public law spheres. It governs all the issues of the form and content of a specific joint activity of individuals pursuing one common legally enforceable goal. Based on this observation there is no reason whatever to doubt, as to which law to apply to private law relations burdened with a foreign element (a foreign corporation) closely connected with a separate legal order. Corporations may never have double or multiple nationality.[92]

Thus far *lex societatis* is the main conflict of law principle of private international law of corporations in all and any actions affecting the legal status of a corporation as a subject of law in general and private international law in particular. Its importance is unquestionable because at any time it gives a perfect answer to the question as to what law to apply to a corporation as a subject of a cross-border activity in a predictable manner for a home state and incorporators. That is the manner advancing specific national corporate law practices in different parts of the world.

This conflict of law principle has always been assumed as playing a particular role in the ruling of cross-border corporate relations and other relations closely connected with them based on the following properties:
- it rests on the very idea of a corporation vested with distinct legal status in one state to which it is subjected throughout its corporate life whenever it carries out a commercial and non-commercial activity directly in this or any other state; and a nature of the problem which may arise with reference to this;
- it provides for predictable conflict of law regulation to ensure unity and integrity of corporations.

When speaking about corporate relations we cannot ignore investment and labour relations as two separate types of contractual relations, on which a corporation as a peculiar legal phenomenon is founded.

3.3.   Particulars of the use of *lex loci*

This section reviews two supplementary phenomena of a socio-economic life of each community ensuring its sustainable growth. These are labour and property as the foundation of all wealth and its sustainable augmentation in relevant communities ensuring their sanctity through distinct fields of private and public law.

---

[92] In the very same way, corporations may not be without any nationality (or in Latin be *ex lege*).

There is nothing in the world more constructive and honourable than labour, especially where there is unequal distribution of property. In this sense, labour is viewed as the origination of property, which right is reckoned to be of the greatest value, importance and necessity for all nations around the world.

But there is another sense in which labour plays a role. There is no better means to keep order inside a separate community and to support those living in it than to give them work on just and fair conditions. In doing so states settle safety, social and economic problems within the society.

This is mainly because payable labour (manual, mechanical or any other kind) is the key to the long-term prosperity of individuals. In the face of the theory of law that is the transformation of an individual into a subject of law, a subject of private law relations and finally into a subject of private international law relations as the most progressive stage of execution of positive rights conferred by sovereign states.

Goods for our markets cannot be made without labour, which substantially increases their value from raw material to product. Labour relations are voluntary and mutually beneficial relations of the parties pursuing different goals. These are:

(1) employees (individuals) having particular financial interest in such relations, which advance commercial and non-commercial business of employers; and

(2) employers (commercial and non-commercial private or public law corporations), which business rests on labour and property.[93]

They have long ceased to be purely national, and in line with other relations arising in a private law sphere at present are characterized by strong legal bonds with distinct systems of law and jurisdictions appearing in foreign subjects (foreign employees or employers) or foreign objects (e.g. material result of works done by employees to employers abroad).

Cross-border labour relations take another specific form. That is an employment contract or a service agreement, under which terms employees (individuals) become bound to employers (legal or physical persons) for remuneration to be given for specific services and works requiring corresponding skills and experience from employees. This specific nature of private law relations induces peculiar public law obligations of employers

---

[93] The very same idea is given in the judgment of the Supreme Court of the UK in *Cox v Ministry of Justice* [2016] UKSC 10 dealing with law of vicarious liability in particular cases having essential elements of labour relations to be governed by proper law.

towards employees as to their pension and social security at the place of rendering these services.

There is also another issue immediately distinguishing cross-border labour relations from other private law relations into which corporations enter. That is the responsibility of employees for services and works done under employment contracts. It is traditionally limited by the sum of remuneration to be paid to employees, which should not be less than the minimum rate set at the place of rendering these services or making works.

Taking into account all these particulars originating from a peculiar nature of these relations, in which the place of services rendering directly affects their character, it has never been a difficult task to choose a rule fit for their proper treatment. That is mainly because, in line with all the other private law activity, a cross-border labour activity results in definite material and non-material effects having "legal seat" in distinct states and jurisdictions. This triggers the application of appropriate private international law rules. That is *lex loci* - a conflict of law principle, which answers the question as to which law will govern labour rights and obligations arising in private law relations closely connected with two or more states.

But an issue arises as to which law will govern peripatetic employment, when the place of work changes. To answer this question it is not enough to take a look at the particular wording of labour rights and obligations given in the relevant contractual documents. It is also necessary to uncover the true nature of specific employment relations the parties entered into, their aim and effect showing to which state these relations are substantially related in traditional terms of conflict of laws rules.

This issue is treated by the court practice[94] covered by the term "an overwhelmingly closer connection with a state", which unveils the extent of connection of private international law relations brought to court with one particular state to show that:
(1) it is more enduring than others; and
(2) without it these relations would not be arranged, treated and executed in a way as it was done.

To respond to this test of an overwhelmingly closer connection with a state, a number of factors should be examined and properly weighed by a court in each particular case. This combination of factors is always peculiar to a private international law case, which may not always fit into fixed formula of national law rules. But sometimes the answer is directly given in public

---

[94] For example, see *Lawson v Serco Ltd [2006]* ICR 250.

law rules of acts having force of national law and resolving this issue in a particular for a situation way making it a matter of this or that law.[95]

As to governance of corporations when we speak of labour rights and obligations we mean in particular:

- rights to directly manage a corporation or delegate its management to other persons for the appropriate salary, to hold office for a definite period of time, to represent a corporation in any and all court proceedings and protest against removal and liability etc.;
- obligations to run a corporation with reasonable care, skill and diligence within the confines of the law; in all transactions of corporations to avoid conflicts of interest and thus exercise independent and professional judgment etc.[96]

These labour rights and obligations being governed by this or that law[97] closely connected with private law relations, means that this law will decide the scope and duration of these rights and obligations.

The use of this conflict of law principle is of note in that it singles out as the only proper connection with a peculiar legal order the one that an individual has with the place in which the value to goods (in a broad sense) is added when this connection is characterized as firm and stable. Otherwise, these private international law relations will be governed by a national law of a

---

[95] Thus, by virtue of the Coalition Provisional Authority Order 17, which entered into force on the date of its signature and still being in force for the duration of the mandate authorizing the MNF under UN Security Council Resolutions 1511 and 1546, the personnel of coalition forces in Iraq, is *"immune from Iraqi legal process"*, for it is recognized in this act that it is *"subject to the exclusive jurisdiction of their Sending States"* and *"immune from local criminal, civil and administrative jurisdiction"*, which nevertheless may be waived, if granted in writing to this effect. This immunity from the jurisdiction of national courts as well as other privileges granted to Coalition forces may evidence of the restoration of capitulation regime (in French – *le régime des capitulations*). That is the old international law regime advanced by Ottoman Empire in the fifteenth century AD and then widely spread around the world.

[96] These issues are governed by *lex loci* when they are not mentioned in a corporate contract. Otherwise, they are governed by *lex societatis* of a corporation as law closely and substantially connected with a corporation, terms of its formation, representation, reorganization, insolvency and termination, which should always be considered in the way advanced by the theory of unity advocating a distinct approach in conflict of law regulation of cross-border corporate and other relations closely connected with them.

[97] That is the law of the place of rending labour services or holding office coinciding with the place where this office is registered.

corporation. This conflict of law principle may serve as a universal principle, because it properly serves private and public interests.

When these goods (and their labour) are brought to foreign markets they appear to be the subject matter of other private law relations accompanied by transfer of property. These are purchase and sale relations of a specific nature, character and form peculiar to the place to which law they are submitted. The holding of property is premised on the idea of unlimited power or dominion of persons over it. Therefore property is wholly subordinated to its holders exercising free will over its fate and correspondingly to their law (in Latin - *lex personalis* or *lex societatis* so far as relevant).

Nevertheless, at the time of free irregular cross-border movements of persons accompanied by transfer of goods, services and technologies, the law applicable to a person may not properly accommodate protection of rights and interests of this property holder's as well as other persons concerned (e.g. purchasers, trustees). Besides there are certain situations, when allocation of property in an illegitimate system of law and jurisdiction may trigger infringement of public interests of states closely and substantially connected with it. That is, for example, in case of the contract of sale to a foreigner of real estate having a particular cultural, religious, scientific or military value for the state with which territory it is inextricably connected and to which system of law and courts it is submitted.[98]

All actions relevant to this type of property are considered by courts of the state, in which it is placed. Under private international law acts that is the exclusive jurisdiction of national courts to hear and determine all such actions[99] based on directly applicable national law rules.

In Russia that is the rule of Art. 1213 of the Civil Code of the Russian Federation in which it is explicitly emphasized that "contracts relating to plots of land, tracts of sub-soil and other immovable property located on the territory of the Russian Federation shall be subjected to Russian law". That is

---

[98] States extend their sovereignty over all persons and things within their territories. Where this property is placed and with which territory this property is closely connected (land, buildings etc.) may decide what is the status of this property, whether this property may be transferred to the ownership of other persons and settle all other issues concerned.

[99] See Art. 98a of the SFAPIL 1987 "...*the court at the domicile or at the registered office of the defendant or the court at the place where the cultural property is located has jurisdiction to entertain actions for recovery within the meaning of Art. 9 of the Act on the Transfer of Cultural Property of 20 June 2003*".

the law establishing rights and obligations in property as well as essential terms of contracts giving rise to them, their arrangement, execution, amendment and termination and affecting the status of this property. By virtue of Art. 1192 of the given legal act this rule precludes the very conflict of law problem for which settlement specific legal means are needed.

The very same rules may be found in other systems of law. For example, in France it is kept that "...immovables are governed by French law even when owned by aliens".[100] Besides all disputes arising in this respect shall be submitted solely (exclusively) to a court of the state where this property is placed (in Latin - *forum rei sitae*). In the legislation of the Czech Republic it is provided that "...only Czech courts or other competent Czech public authorities may decide on rights to real estate, which are in the Czech Republic...".[101]

The necessary inference from this is that neither can any other conditions be established as to origination, execution and termination of rights to property of general public importance nor can any other rights and obligations in their respect may be granted except for *lex rei sitae* nor can any disputes with respect to these issues may be heard and determined in any other place than in *forum rei sitae*.

Thus, in particular private law cases, in disputes over the fate of relevant things[102] (individual or corporate property as the case may be), to which much importance is given at this time, a conflict of law rule referring to the law of the state where this property is placed (in Latin – *lex rei sitae*) may give a clue to a list of private law issues, notwithstanding the fact that these things are under the power and dominion of persons and thus should be subjected to their law (in Latin - *lex personalis* or *lex societatis*). All these issues governed by a conflict of law principle *lex loci* fall into the following two categories comprising:

as to status of property:

–   things, which may or may never be subject of property;

---

[100]   See Art. 3 of FCC 2013.

[101]   See Para 68, Title VII "Real rights" of Law on Private International Law of the Czech Republic, No. 91/2012.

[102]   The fact is that states give different names to things as per their characteristics and significance for a definite community, which carry special legal consequences with them. Their classification also differs and not without reason. These may be movable and immovable things, fungible and non-fungible things, consumable and non-consumable things, divisible and non-divisible things. To all these terms which may employ different words, sovereign states may ascribe different meanings in accordance with general or specific qualities of things.

- persons, who may have or may never have a capacity to own specific property;

as to rights to property:

- origination, execution and termination of rights to property;
- modes of origination and termination of rights (voluntary and involuntary acts - free will of parties, renunciation, expiration of time, destruction of property);
- perfectness or imperfectness of origination and termination of rights;
- validity and invalidity of rights;
- formal evidence of rights to property;
- scope of these rights;
- legal effect of acquisition, sale and transfer of individual or corporate property;
- other consequences attached to exercising absolute or relative rights to property;
- remedies allowed to protect absolute or relative rights to property;
- causes of the loss of property.

Therefore we may conclude that this conflict of law principle has no other end than that to refer the exercising of rights to individual or corporate property to the state closely connected with it. That is the state in which property has its real seat (in Latin – *situs*). The latter is determined by law enforcers based on general and specific properties of things existing independently from our perception but submitted to it for the purposes of classification, which we make herewith.

Based on it, all things fall into the following main categories:
(1) movable and immovable things;
(2) fungible and non-fungible things;
(3) consumable and non-consumable things;
(4) divisible and non-divisible things;
(5) negotiable and non-negotiable things.

With respect to all these categories of things different formulations of the conflict of law principle are employed. They display specific ideas on these things and their appearance considered by both jurists and practitioners of law for the further incorporation into the practice of private law regulation.

Thus, for example, the law of the place in which the public (trade or commercial) register (im)movable, non-fungible, non-consumable, (non)divisible and negotiable things are entered or the law of the actual place of movable, fungible, consumable, (non)divisible and negotiable things, when the relevant legal act or fact takes place. This law will govern essential terms of contracts as instruments employed by legal theory and practice to create, change and terminate rights and obligations in property affecting its status.

Hence, it means that whenever there is a private international law dispute over corporate property having qualities of the above-mentioned things,[103] rights to this property as well as other private law issues form a part of the state into which public (commercial or trade) register it is entered[104] to ensure interests of incorporators and cover commercial and other risks of the corporate activity.[105]

In each specific private international law dispute brought to court special attention should be paid to particulars of civil, corporate, investment and other private law relations the parties entered into to create, change or terminate rights in property with cross-border impact. Among these particulars are the nature and qualities of property affecting the legal form and essential terms of contracts as well as other details of private law relations. This all exerts a strong influence on the choice of applicable law and jurisdiction. Dealing with this matter means to clarify the scope and extent of conflict of law principles, which may be of a value for the settlement of a private international law dispute and determine which courts are empowered to hear and determine it.

Apart from cross-border labour and property relations on which corporate law activity rests, the private international law effect of permanent establishment by corporations abroad should also be mentioned. That is when an activity requires mandatory registration in foreign states and jurisdictions of overseas branches of corporations for tax and other purposes of host states. The main idea is that to enter new markets foreign companies should open overseas branches, which only then shall be considered as legally effective, when they are kept in accordance with mandatory or default material law rules of all these foreign states.

This activity changes labour and property relations between a corporation and foreign states' jurisdictions to render services or make works through

---

[103] In particular cases that is the state, based on which law protection of intellectual property rights is demanded.

[104] This register is traditionally held by competent persons of a home state except for overseas branch registers.

[105] Keeping in mind a particular nature of corporations largely resting on the shared property, a corporate contract is the main source of origination, exercising and termination of rights of the corporate property. As a result all the issues concerned with formation, implementation, amendment and termination of this contract shall be exclusively governed by national law of a corporation as law determining its legal status in the private international law sphere.

the relevant legal forms set up and being run under material law rules of host states. All types of the permanent activity by corporations through overseas branches are structured into distinct legal forms revealing a specific nature of private law relations, into which corporations enter with the aim to make profit in separate spheres of the socio-economic life of relevant communities. The law governing all these distinct forms of private law relations is the law of the place where a contract or any other legal arrangement is made.[106]

Another consideration is: why does it matter under private international law, which form private international law relations will have? There is a direct relationship between form of legal relations and their content. And not without reason. For the activity to be effected, it should receive a definite content. This content is given when this activity takes a definite form.

Law is the formal instrument of social regulation based on the balance or equilibrium of rights and duties. As a result only form determines the scope of rights, obligations and responsibility of the parties. When viewed through the prism of private international law that is the form of the state closely and/or substantially connected with private law relations. With respect to a particular character of private law contracts that is the law of the place, where this contract is made (in Latin – *lex loci contractus*). From the view of the essence that is the law of the place where parties reached agreement on essential terms of a private law deal and put it into the form prescribed by governing law.

Rules of *lex loci contractus* cannot be avoided by the parties for the particular interest underlying them. That is the public interest transforming them from the category of mandatory rules, which cannot be derogated by the consent of the parties, to directly applicable material law rules precluding the very problem of conflicting regulatory interests in the private law sphere. But what should be noted as well is that in separate cases this form may be

---

[106] In the present context it should be pointed out that the meaning of the terms "contract" and "agreement" differs depending on a jurisdiction. For example, in the Kingdom of Bhutan "...*every promise and every set of promises forming the consideration for each other shall be an "agreement". An agreement shall amount to a contract and shall be enforceable at law if it is made with the free consent of competent parties for a lawful consideration and for a lawful object and is not declared to be void or illegal by this Act or by any other law in force in the Kingdom of Bhutan*".

submitted to the law of the place where the private international law deal has to be executed or some other law.[107]

As a general rule characterization of facts around specific types of private international law relations as those constituting tort and delict is a matter of law of the forum. Only the court of the forum may definitely conclude that there is a trespass or any other tort, in particular, "affecting immovable property"[108] in actions of the parties of contractual and extra contractual relations and decide to which law this tort should be submitted.

From the general course of private international law we know that disputes of cross-border corporate relations and other relations closely connected with them are submitted to *lex loci*. These are private international law rights and obligations arising out of cross-border corporate and other relations closely connected with them. Hearings of these disputes are guided by the law of the place where the tort or delict from contractual and extra contractual obligations occurred. The rationale for this is as follows: what really matters in face of law and practice of conflict of law regulation is that there is a strong connection between the breach of contractual or extra contractual duty and the territory of the state, where this breach occurred. That is the place where the party suffered loss or inconvenience from this breach.

It thus appears that if there is no other factor to displace *lex loci delicti*, no other law may guide these private international law relations when brought to the appropriate court. The potential factors are elements of events constituting the tort or delict in question each tending to a separate national public order.[109] These factors may relate to:

(1) parties of a separate private international law dispute brought to court;

---

[107] For the evidence, see Art. 7 of the TAPIPL 2007, in which it is stipulated that *"legal transactions may be carried out pursuant to the form being in conformity with the provisions prescribed by substantial law in accordance with the laws of the place of their execution or by the law applicable to the substance of the said legal transaction".*

[108] See Art. 30 of the Civil Jurisdiction and Judgments Act, 1982.

[109] In that instance, under UK legislation, *"where elements of those events occur in different countries, the applicable law under the general rule is to be taken as being – (a) for a cause of action in respect of personal injury caused to an individual or death resulting from personal injury, the law of the country where the individual was when he sustained the injury; (b) for a cause of action in respect of damage to property, the law of the country where the property was when it was damaged; and (c) in any other case, the law of the country in which the most significant element or elements of those events occurred"* – see Art. 11 of the Private International Law (Miscellaneous Provisions) Act 1995.

(2) all and any or particular circumstances around these events;

(3) all and any or particular consequences of these events for the parties.

In each particular case the court resolves a conflict of law problem brought before them based on the intention to submit this case or a separate private law issue from this case to proper law (in Latin – *lex causae*). Therefore it is sufficiently recognized that when, based on one or a combination of factors, connecting events (which constitute the tort or delict) with this or that state and this connection becomes overwhelmingly stronger than any other connection, the law of this particular state will guide private international law relations in a specific for this state way.

This may be:

(1) law of nationality / domicile / habitual residence of the damaged party;

(2) law of the state where the workplace or nationality / domicile/ habitual residence of the damaging party is;

(3) law of the state where the damage occurred or any other law.

And considering that private international law of all states traditionally distinguishes between three main matters[110] which substance varies along a number of lines, this problem may be settled distinctly depending on the place of the forum where distinct meaning and value is given to facts of each particular case.

However, this failure to do what is required under governing law with respect to contractual or extra contractual relations may be both wilful and negligent. The degree of culpability in each specific private international law case is irrelevant to conflict of law regulation. It is determined by the court at the relevant proceeding affecting the extent of liability. But what really matters to the law enforcer and the parties involved in the face of this particular legal institute of private international law, is the allocation of different forms of dishonest business practice taking different forms (unfair competition, unjust enrichment etc.) in the proper system of law for the further choice of appropriate remedies.

When dealing with unfair competition it seems to be clear that what interests a law enforcer the most is what market has been effected by unfair

---

[110] These are matters of public interest as well as matters of substance and procedure based on three-fold jurisprudence developed in detail in the present paper. The same idea is given in the judgement in *Ministry of Defence v Iraqi Civilians [2016]* UKSC 25.

competition in distinct socio-economic spheres when this act is enveloped into different forms.[111]

When addressing issue of unjust enrichment to the national legislation, depending on the state of the forum it is governed by the law:
(1) under which the transfer of assets in favour of the enriched person took place;[112]
(2) applicable to the existing transactions or where the unjust enrichment has occurred;[113]
(3) which governs the legal relationship, either existing or assumed, on the basis of which the enrichment occurred or of the state in which the enrichment occurred;
(4) of the forum, if the parties agreed to apply to this law[114] etc.

In the latter case Swiss courts will hear the cases if it is the place of domicile, habitual residence or the place of business of the defendant.[115] By virtue of the theory of vested rights advanced in the private international law sphere corporations are deemed to be domiciled in states vesting them with distinct corporate law rights and obligations to be exercised in territories of their jurisdiction or effective control.

Having expounded the scope of *lex loci* regulation and it is possible to classify cases to which this conflict of law principle applies. These are:
(1) terms of employment and liability of the parties to labour contracts to be governed by law of the place of employment (*lex loci laboris*);

---

[111] Thus, if, for example, that is an act or practice in the course of industrial or commercial activity that results in the breach of Ghanaian law or international or regional obligation to which a person involved in business or commercial activity in Ghana is subjected, and in a manner contrary to honest business practice constitutes an act of unfair competition, all and any demands resulting from this act are a matter of Ghanaian law.

As to this it is interesting to note that under the law of Ghana, unfair competition may take forms of 1) causing confusion with respect to another's enterprise or its activity; 2) damaging another person's goodwill or reputation; 3) misleading the public; 4) discrediting the public; 5) unfair competition in respect of secret information; 6) unfair competition in respect of national and international obligations (see Protection Against Unfair Competition Act. 2000, No. 589).

[112] See Art. 10 of SCC 2009.

[113] See Art. 38 of the TAPIPL 2007.

[114] See Art. 128 of the SFAPIL 1987.

[115] See Art. 127 of the SFAPIL 1987.

(2) status of property as well as corresponding rights and obligations of the parties to be submitted to law of the state, where this property is placed (*lex rei sitae*);

(3) form and content of a definite obligation in particular or a legal act in general to be governed by law of the place, where they are made (*lex loci actus/lex loci celebrationis/lex loci contractus*);

(4) legal effect or consequence of legal acts to be dealt with by law of the place, where this act or effect occurred (*lex loci actus/lex contractus/lex loci delicti commissi*).

To complete this observation of mainly mandatory conflict of law principles (*lex personalis*, *lex societatis* and *lex loci*) it is noteworthy that they all fall into two main categories. These are subjective (*lex societatis* and *lex personalis*) and objective conflict of law principles (*lex loci*). The line of separation lies in the very nature of connection or legal bonds with a foreign state. All these principles are well developed in the private international law theory and practice. And as the practice shows there have never been problems with their use when resolving the endless diversity of legal problems arising in cross-border corporate and other relations closely connected with them.

3.4.   Particulars of the use of *lex voluntatis*

Admitting a strictly determinate character of a cross-border commercial and non-commercial activity of corporations requiring corresponding conflict of law rules as well as other legal rules (directly applicable rules and rules on international jurisdiction) in the sphere of private international law, it is worth highlihgting a sphere of individual freedom, to which a very considerable room is given in different states. It is assigned by sovereign states that advance the idea that not all legal provisions striving for peace and order inside distinct communities may be observed by the use of legal force or coercion.

These are to a great extent issues pertaining to personal economic (financial) interests of private law subjects, which are predominant in the corporate law sphere. To deal with them sovereign states confer properly advised parties of comparable bargaining power with rights to opt applicable law and jurisdiction for more favourable or predictable terms of disputes resolution. Because they are commonly considered as the best judges in all and any disputes arising out of cross-border contractual and extra contractual relations as to effect of these relations in general and specific consequences of breaches in particular.[116]

With respect to corporate law that is the sphere in which an association of persons conferred with a number of distinct corporate law rights is perceived as that having and expressing its own "will". That is the one resting on the idea of inevitable subjectivity in the exercise of the choice of types and forms of a corporate activity as a range of distinct legal possibilities granted by a sovereign state to individuals.

This is regardless of the fact that this issue is handled by individuals authorized to undertake commercial and non-commercial transactions on behalf of "soulless persons" (corporations) to create definite legal obligations distinct from those of individuals. These persons include subjects of a private law activity as commercial and non-commercial corporations. Their activity initially rests on the idea of free will of incorporators contracting a specific legal status for a particular financial (economic) interest, because this status gives them certain privileges, freedoms and immunities in the risk-taking activity, in particular, against debts and other obligations to be taken by corporations.

And with respect to a cross-border activity it has to be noted that both in corporate law and private international law of corporations the theory of will receives development peculiar to these distinct spheres of social regulation:

First, in both spheres a subjective will when it is supported by an objective will (that is the one inherent to sovereigns states) is called "legal right", "legal interest", "privilege", "power" or "immunity" as the case may be.

Second, the substance of this right or freedom depends on the sphere of social regulation. As a rule the general term "right" or "freedom" in its traditional acceptation embracing a legal right, a legal interest, a power, a privilege and immunity has always been associated with the dignity of independence. It is different from the right itself in the narrow meaning of this term and when viewed from the standpoint of corporate law that is the independence in arranging and exercising a corporate activity in a peculiar

---

[116] It is pretty obvious to observe that the term "comparable bargaining power" embraces all and any sort of equilibrium between interests, rights and freedoms of two or more distinct private law subjects. It is presumed when 1) parties further their uncommon goals perfectly attainable by legal means chosen by them; 2) no one takes a dominant position when drafting contractual provisions to guide their relations to a specific end or choosing law and jurisdiction to treat all and any controversies arising between them.

manner. That is the one stipulated in national corporate law when this activity is carried out inside a distinct community or private international law of corporations dealing with legal and jurisdictional problems in the corporate sphere when this activity has a cross-border impact.

These issues of corporate free will are relevant to:
- choice of the place where to establish / re-establish a corporation, when its incorporators intend to abandon strict bounds of the national legislation;
- right of selecting of the appropriate corporate law form from a great number of forms accompanied by the closure of numerous corporate law issues (the main end, name, address of a corporation, sum of the charter capital etc.);
- exercise of the choice with respect to the management scheme (one-tier, two-tier systems of management etc.);
- appointment of persons to manage a corporate activity;
- choice of the state in which to open banking accounts necessary for commercial or non-commercial corporations to make financial operations;
- choice of the currency in which to envelope these financial operations;
- right to change or terminate a corporate activity whenever incorporators wish.

It is understood that these are corporate law issues left to the free will of individuals to decide whether to take certain corporate actions or refrain from taking or doing them within definite strictly set limits.

In the sphere of private international law of corporations the freedom of the parties to incorporate and other contracts closely connected with them distinguishes between two distinct forms having distinct legal effect:
- choice of the system of law giving most favourable for the parties terms of doing commercial and non-commercial business;
- choice of the court system to deal with all and any real and good faith controversies, which may ever arise between the parties in a predictable and cost-effective way.

They are grounded upon two distinct theories (party autonomy and forum shopping) and employ different legal means. Nevertheless, there is one thing in common by which they may be compared. They pursue the idea that is likely to give parties entering into these relations for a common economic (financial) or any other interest the right to guide them or treat all or a part of legal or factual issues arising in their respect in a predictable or more favourable for them way.

When reviewing the legal feasibility of this choice of law and jurisdiction, it soon becomes apparent that it may be made by the parties at the very arrangement of contractual relations or at any time later provided that the exercise of this choice does not adversely affect third parties' rights and/or any other rights as the main condition of its validity.[117] With respect to the scope of this choice, these are all and any potential and/or existing private law disputes placed in the hands of judges in anticipation of the final decision on a particular case brought before the court when nothing may be changed or take effect.

To take effect this choice should be structured in a particular form, which is a prior written agreement for the prorogation of jurisdiction and/or choice of applicable law. In particular cases this choice may be considered as exercised if it results in certainty from contractual provisions or from the study of circumstances around particular cross-border corporate law cases.

The choice of law in this prior written agreement of the parties may not suggest an exercised choice of the forum. A good example of this comes from the text of the State Immunity Act 1978 enacted by the Queen Elizabeth II, a mere provision in any agreement that the state is to be governed by the law of the United Kingdom (prorogation / derogation clause / agreement) is not to be regarded as a submission of the state (public corporations) to jurisdiction of courts of the UK.

The theory upon which this rule is grounded is the one advanced in the private international law sphere in numerous legal systems. That is the theory of conflict of law rules employed by national courts apart from international jurisdiction rules in private law issues burdened with foreign

---

[117] See Art. 6 of the SCC 2009, which keeps that *"the voluntary exclusion of applicable law and the waiver of any rights acknowledged therein shall only be valid when they do not contradict the public interest or public policy or cause a detriment to third parties"*. Thus, as it comes from the text of this rule, this choice of applicable law should not infringe interests of the state closely and substantially connected with cross-border relations in the private law sphere. And at this observation it is interesting and important to note that the concept of public interest advanced in Spanish legislation in line with a modern trend around the world, does not embrace interests of third parties. They are mentioned in this rule but considered independently of the idea of the public interest, including also public policy. But as it may be seen, in this rule a Spanish lawmaker directs our attention to issues, which are most likely to refer to the choice of governing or applicable law, rather public interest affecting its validity. The very same idea is given in Art. 4 of the PAPIL 2011, in which it is stipulated that *"...the choice of law made after the legal relationship has arisen shall not violate third party rights"*.

elements. The principle use which states make of these rules is to apply material law rules of the state closely connected with these relations. It differs from the one pertaining to international jurisdiction rules ensuring submission of these relations to appropriate jurisdiction. And this difference appears to have been fundamental.

On a number of issues, sovereign states ensure freedom in submission of private international law cases to one particular system of law and exclusive jurisdiction of the relevant court based on the sound foundation. It brings order and predictability in exercising private law relations across borders of states saving time and money of those being in dispute.

The idea of freedom in this sphere *historically* owes much of its intrinsic value to the natural idea of freedom in the complete signification of this unique social phenomenon. That is the freedom initially granted by God to a man as a number of natural rights limited by a number of duties known as Ten Commandments of God to ensure their full power over all things and actions in this material world. This natural idea was correspondingly adopted by states in different spheres of positive law and jurisprudence but this time advancing a two-tier model of particular social regulation.

That is the model, which is likely to persist unchanged as long as it is needed, being grounded upon the idea of good faith with rights, legal interests, power, privileges and immunities on one side and duties and liability in private and public interests on the other side. It is particularly formulated and employed in different systems of law giving rise to distinct subjects of private and public law. In the corporate law sphere it is the idea of national corporate law constructs asynchronously advanced in these distinct systems of law to confer private law subjects with particular scope of rights and obligations.

In private international law this freedom has always rested on:

(1) the idea of ultimate importance and inviolability of a contract (when it does not run counter public interest of one particular state, with which private law relations are overwhelmingly connected) as a non-exclusive form of a private law activity; as well as

(2) the idea of sanctity of property and other rights conferred by states as a substance of private law relations, because form and substance have always been considered in unity, which is likely to be necessary for predictable execution of private international law relations.

And this freedom or right to designate law and jurisdiction keeping legal and jurisdictional problems from arising in private international law disputes of the parties shall be perceived as exercised in accordance with good faith then and only then, when:

(1) there is consent to submit private law relations or their part tending to distinct legal orders to material law and judicial/administrative authority of one particular state closely and sufficiently connected with them;[118]

(2) there is evidence of meeting of wills to this effect in a specific legitimate external form of prorogation/derogation clauses/agreements.[119]

Judges decide whether the consent of the parties is voluntary and sufficient to settle a conflict of law and jurisdiction problem in a prescribed a manner. If so and the choice correspondingly made by the parties is not random, it takes effect leaving aside jurisdictional and legal problems. In this the parties' will is transformed into a deed, which cannot be undone by the subsequent unilateral denial or claim of non-performance of specific contractual obligations to distinct material law and forum. The same is true for the legal consequences they are accompanied with, and terms of invalidation of these obligations and other private international law issues.

However, should this agreement become void and as a consequence this choice of law and forum ineffective, judges of the state closely and substantially connected with a private international law dispute will be called upon to search for governing law (be it national or foreign law) based on conflict of law principles preserved in national law acts.

Nevertheless, there is a good list of issues excluded from the scope of parties' volition. As a general rule the choice of law / forum made freely by the parties cannot be put forward in particular private international law cases and their effect *"pour des motifs d'ordre public"*. In other words, if this may have a direct negative impact on public interest of the state closely and substantially connected with them.

There is probably no private international law doctrine of the same weight in national legal systems as the doctrine of public order. It was commonly and universally accepted mainly (but not exclusively) in prohibitive legal rules entered into a national law system as rules overriding all other rules applicable to legal relations with a foreign element in the sphere of private international law regulation. This doctrine rests on the idea that laws, customs and traditions on which sovereign states are built, should always be

---

[118] Without this consent duly made under governing law there is no agreement to the effect to submit private law relations to particular law and jurisdiction.

[119] This legitimacy of the form is determined by mandatory legal rules of the state closely and substantially connected with private law relations. That is law of the place, where a contract is made (in Latin - *lex loci contractus*) prescribing for the manner in which this consent we are speaking about, should be given.

kept, because there is nothing more important and valuable than the sovereign will and interests of the peoples constituting legitimate states.[120]

Issues generally excluded from the scope of parties' volition are:

(1) capacity to act and other unequivocal criteria for the validity of a contract;

(2) essential terms of separate types of contracts exclusively governed by law closely connected with private international law relations (in Latin - *lex causae*);

(3) other essential conditions opposing to the very nature of a particular private law agreement.

It is easy to see the reason for removing them from the sphere of individual freedom. These are the interests of states to establish conditions for the unrestricted exercise of civil/commercial rights on a cross-border basis, which do not directly fall under the category of public interests but are closely connected with them.

In summary, there is a particular area of freedom in the private international law sphere, identified by signs of stability, firmness and immutability. These are all characteristics responding exactly to the needs of the cross-border trade and commerce. However, when this freedom directly opposes to the freedom and independence of sovereign states taking form of public policy, public health and public security, for which communities have struggled over the centuries, it cannot come into being.

Thus far we have collected and arranged a number of conflict of law principles making up a separate legal institute of private international law dealing with legal problems arising in the corporate law sphere on a cross-border basis. These are conflict of law principles governing civil, commercial and corporate law issues by going to the very heart of these issues and resting on distinct private law ideas:

(1) *lex personalis* - to business-to-consumer contracts;

(2) *lex societatis* – to corporate law relations; and

(3) *lex loci* or *lex voluntatis* – to commercial relations etc.

In reply to the issue as to whether unequal value is assigned to them it should be noted that their effect differs along many lines. For example, the main distinction between *lex societatis* and other conflict of law principles advanced in the corporate law sphere consists in that it takes a more tenable position for the following characteristics:

---

[120] Sometimes these interests may oppose sovereign interests of other states ensuring its keeping on a safe side for them. In these cases the following maxim should guide them in the right direction - "*quod tibi non vis fieri, alteri ne feceris*".

- proper reflection of the nature of corporateness suggesting particular regulation;
- determination with certainty of law applicable to relations on formation, reorganization, insolvency and termination of corporations so as to ensure unity of all and any corporate actions affecting the status of corporations;
- certain practical reasons underlying this choice to the exclusion of any other connection than the single connection with a home state of a corporation with respect to the effect of this law operation.

That is the particular nature of cross-border corporate relations and other relations closely connected with them suggesting a wide range of private international law issues arising in this sphere to be dealt with in a manner ensuring their unity and integrity.

This means that all these conflict of law principles should always be considered as a whole. It is necessary to make private international law of corporations keep pace with ever-changing circumstances largely affecting legal status of corporations as distinct subjects of law as well as particular character and effect of cross-border risk-taking transactions they enter into.

3.5. International jurisdiction over cross-border corporate disputes and other disputes closely connected with them (cause, particulars and effect)

The choice of law would be pointless if there were no courts within which to decide and enforce the distinct substantive issues at trial. Only courts decide on all and any controversies and differences between corporations and other subjects of law in their commercial and non-commercial activity with cross-border impact. Also, only court decisions give us a complete picture of the struggle for the proper law in each particular case.

For this reason in order to show the true scope of private international law of corporations, we need to deal with another very important private international law issue. That is the international jurisdiction (in French – *la jurisdiction internationale*) of national courts[121] on civil law issues burdened with foreign elements and thus leading to conflicts of national law and jurisdiction.

---

[121] That is the jurisdiction of national courts and other national authorities in a broad list of private international law matters. Hence, it means that the autonomous institutions (e.g. international arbitration) dealing with private international law disputes on the basis of the consent of the parties are excluded from the present survey adverting to national systems of law and courts for the settlement of legal and jurisdictional problems arising in the private law sphere.

These are rather those civil law issues specifically relating to the area of private international law of corporations arising *ex contractu* or *ex delicto*, dealt with through the settlement of conflicts of prescriptive and enforcement jurisdictions:

− membership in national and foreign corporate and unincorporated bodies etc.;
− ownership, possession and use of individual and corporate property under cross-border business-to-consumer and business-to-business contracts;
− use of patents, trade-marks and other intellectual rights in cross-border commercial transactions;
− main effect of cross-border employment and consumer relations;
− injuries (death and personal) and damage to property when rendering labour and other services on a cross-border basis etc.

Earlier we have already discussed main principles of conflict of law regulation of private international law relations resting on the very idea of necessity to find law closely or substantially connected with these relations in order to rule them. The very same idea is employed in legal issues concerned with a choice of appropriate forum in which defendants are bound to answer on particulars of private international law deals.

In England, as a general rule, to establish private law rights and obligations for a forum to be deemed appropriate there should be:

• an available head of jurisdiction; and
• the relevant court within which competence this or that private law dispute is brought considers it as an appropriate one.

And the first issue arising in this observation is what falls under the scope of the term "jurisdiction".

We know that "jurisdiction" as a general term has always been considered as legal power to govern or exercise authority within distinct territorial boundaries or as the extent of sovereign power to make legal decisions and/or judgments on all and any issues arising in public and private law spheres with extra-territorial effect (as a more particular term). This term is closely connected with a notion of sovereignty making up an integral attribute of a separate strictly functional and politically independent community (a state) extending its power and force over a separate territory, within which bounds this power is deemed to be supreme.

In this meaning the term "jurisdiction" is used in national law acts conferring national courts with necessary power to hear and determine all and any cases falling under the purview of the relevant state.[122] This observation is particularly important because it has always been held that the consent of the parties may neither set nor change or enlarge jurisdiction of national courts for its execution to the benefit of the private use.

We are speaking of the general benefit of the peoples constituting a distinct community, which the parties cannot determine save for particular cases ensuring steady and harmonious growth of cross-border trade and commerce. For example, Italian courts will neither hear nor determine any actions with respect to foreign immovable property simply because they have no jurisdiction with respect to this.[123]

In the private international law sphere, jurisdiction is the power of national courts to hear and rule disputes burdened with one or a number of determining foreign elements (tending to distinct public orders), and decide all other issues concerned with exercising private international law rights and obligations. This power is granted by supreme laws (constitutions) of sovereign states as well as other acts developing their legal rules in a manner to keep jurisdictional balance between:

(1) national courts of different states by operation of the theory of jurisdiction in international issues, as well as

(2) national courts of one particular state by virtue of principles of federalism and alike advanced in the relevant community.

To hear and determine a case means:

(1) to choose governing or applicable material law rules by operation of conflict of law rules;

(2) to establish the contents of this law or apply the law of the forum, when there is no way to establish the contents of foreign law closely connected with private law relations;[124]

---

[122] Under Serbian Constitution, "...*judicial power shall be unique on the territory of the Republic of Serbia. Courts shall ... perform their duties in accordance with the Constitution, Law and other general acts, when stipulated by the Law, generally accepted rules of international law and ratified international contracts...*" (see Art. 7 of Constitution of the Republic of Serbia adopted by the National Assembly of the Republic of Serbia at its first special session in 2006 held on 30 September 2006).

[123] For the evidence read the following rule of Italian legislation "...*la giurisdizione italiana non sussiste rispetto ad azioni reali aventi ad oggetto beni immobili situati all'estero...*"(Art. 5 of RSIDIP 1995).

[124] The main function of judges charged with resolution of a private international law dispute is to properly observe strict written law in this particular sphere of regulation. These are directly applicable rules, conflict of law rules and

(3) to establish private law rights and obligations of the parties in dispute and thus resolve the dispute.

An explanation is needed of private international law disputes in the corporate sphere. First, these are heavy commercial disputes over all and any contracts, covenants, debts, accounts, trespasses, breaches, losses, grievances and their consequences arising out of a private law activity of corporations permanently placed in different parts of the world and, second, minor corporate property disputes closely connected with two or more sovereign states and their jurisdiction.[125]

To give national courts jurisdiction over the subject matter of private international law disputes means to settle a separate choice of the forum issue in the relevant actions affecting private law rights and obligations of individuals on a cross-border basis. That is the issue arising each time when there is a foreign element in the structure of private law relations (foreign object or subject) tending to a separate public order in which it is originally neatly placed. And this choice is deemed to be properly made when the dominion of a court over persons, actions or things, over which there is a real and good faith private international law dispute, may be evidenced by the operation of national law rules on international jurisdiction or provisions of prorogation / derogation agreements binding their parties to this effect under governing law.[126]

In order to have this dominion over persons, defendants should be closely connected with states of fora. This connection rests on the idea of nationality, domicile, habitual residence or a place of business underlying national law rules on international jurisdiction of national courts to consider private

---

[125] international jurisdiction rules. Judges do not formulate new rules of law to deal with a particular dispute brought before them. That is the function of legislation.

With respect to these observations it is important to stress that when we speak of jurisdiction of national courts, we mean courts of general and special jurisdiction. In the first case, these are national law courts exercising their authority over all and any types of disputes, while in the second, these are administrative, judicial, labour, criminal and other courts advanced in national court systems. Thus, for example, in Luxemburg this issue is settled in the Civil Code (*Code civil*), in Netherlands – in the Code of civil procedure (*Wetboek van Burgerlijke Rechtsvodering*), in Greece – in the Code of civil procedure (*Kwdikaç Politikhç Dikonomiaç*), in Denmark – in the law on civil procedure (*Lov om rettens pleje*).

[126] For further illustration read the Tunisian legislation, which states "...*les juridictions tunisiennes sont compétentes si les parties au litige les désignent comme telles, ou, si le défendeur accepte d'être jugé par elles; sauf si l'objet du litige est un droit réel portant sur un immeuble situé hors du territoire tunisien*" (art. 4 of PILC 1998).

international law cases. These are rules advancing the idea of dominion or power of national courts of the place where persons (physical or legal) permanently live and make business and have intention to continue doing that in the very same way, which is found to be acceptable for sovereign states.

Thus, for instance, this choice shall be considered as appropriately made with respect to the forum in Switzerland in the event of dissolution of a Swiss registered partnership then and only then, when, first, there is a partnership relationship between the claimant and defendant; and second, the defendant is domiciled in Switzerland. But if such partners have no connection with Switzerland, then Switzerland cannot affect their legal status. So, the forum of the state of partnership registration shall be considered as appropriate to entertain actions or petitions relating to dissolution of a registered partnership.

It follows that to submit a private international law dispute on particular actions and their legal effect to Swiss judicial or administrative authorities, the case should be closely or substantially connected with Switzerland. For this reason it is necessary to assess the choice of the forum facts of each particular case evidencing the court jurisdiction over persons, actions and things, over which there is a private international law dispute. Otherwise, this dispute cannot be heard and determined by these authorities.[127]

Next when examining the particulars of settlement of conflicts of prescriptive and enforcement jurisdictions over employment and consumer contracts it should be said that all and any disputes arising between the parties to these contracts shall be settled:

(1) by the courts of the place where these labour services are rendered standing for the dominion of the court over actions; or

(2) by the courts of the place of nationality (domicile or habitual residence) of the consumer or the party rendering services (making works) under a consumer contract standing for the dominion or power of the court over persons necessary to hear and determine such disputes.

With respect to jurisdiction over effect of employment and consumer relations, all and any private international law conflicts over the death and personal injuries and damage to property arising under these and other contracts into which corporations enter shall be resolved by the court of the place where the event causing the damage occurred.[128] In particular, this

---

[127] See Art. 65b and Art. 3 of the SFAPIL 1987.

[128] By way of illustration see Art. 5 of the PILC 1998, in which it is given that *"...les juridictions tunisiennes connaissent également : 1 - Des actions relatives à la*

court will decide who actually was at fault. Because no person whose rights were breached should be left without appropriate remedy. For liability to be firmly established and thus hold persons (e.g. corporations, employees) responsible for their acts or instructions to acts which were given by them means to apply to a close connection test or a test of representative capacity dealing with the issue as to who is at fault in each particular case and why there is no alternative answer.[129]

In specific circumstances designated by a sovereign state in national law acts parties may agree to exclusive jurisdiction of one particular court over their disputes which have already arisen or may arise with respect to any type of legal relations these parties entered into.[130] Prorogation of jurisdiction is a separate phenomenon in the sphere of private international law. And when viewed through the prism of private international law practice using categories of rights and freedoms, the right of prorogation is the power to opt or choose the forum to resolve all and any private law disputes arising between the parties of corporate and other relations closely connected with them. The only condition one may find in national rules on international jurisdiction is that this should not cause any detriment either to the public interest of a state closely connected with them or private interests of third parties.

In order to have effect this prorogation should be expressly accepted by the parties of private law relations. Hence, it means that the prorogation agreement of the parties should be grounded upon legally binding arrangement, the form of which accords with the practice of making these arrangements set inside a definite community, and the content of which

---

responsabilité civile délictuelle si le fait générateur de responsabilité ou le préjudice est survenu sur le territoire tunisien". The same idea is given in Swiss legislation: "Swiss courts at the place where the event causing the damage occurred have jurisdiction to entertain actions relating to damages…". (Art. 130 of the SFAPIL 1987).

[129] See the case Mr A M Mohamud (in substitution for Mr A Mohamud v WM Morrison Supermarkets plc [2016] UKSC 11; Cox v Ministry of Justice [2016] UKSC 10 dealing with vicarious liability in tort to be imposed on a corporation for the conduct of the individual (employee).

[130] "In materia di giurisdizione volontaria, la giurisdizione sussiste, oltre che nei casi specificamente contemplati dalla presente legge e in quelli in cui è prevista la competenza per territorio di un giudice italiano, quando il provvedimento richiesto concerne un cittadino italiano o una persona residente in Italia o quando esso riguarda situazioni o rapporti ai quali è applicabile la legge italiana" (See Art. 9 RSIDIP 1995). As it may be seen from the above citation, Italian legislation sets terms to which voluntary jurisdiction should respond in order to take effect with respect to a particular private international law case.

advances the underlying public policy considerations of states closely connected with private law relations. The main idea rooted in these agreements is that unequivocal acceptance of the jurisdiction over all and any issues in dispute should be evidenced before proceeding has begun. The easiest way to do this is to demonstrate a signed agreement rather to prove it by the parties conduct.

But there are cases when consent of the parties may not have any effect on submission of private law relations to one particular jurisdiction apart from the one closely and substantially connected with them. We are speaking of exclusive competence assigned to national courts of general jurisdiction over the subject matter of private law disputes particularly sensitive for public policy, public security and public health of states having a legitimate regulatory interest in them.

That is the power of courts to consider actions on a list of issues pertaining to:

(1) corporate nationality (in particular private law issues as to when this nationality is deemed to be granted, acquired or lost as issues inextricably linked with a home state of a corporation);

(2) validity of constitution, nullity or dissolution of corporations or validity of decisions made by their organs;

(3) validity of all and any entries in public (trade/commercial) registers;

(4) registration or validity of patents, trade marks, designs and or other similar rights required to be deposited or registered under the relevant law;

(5) real property rights;

(6) all other issues, which under special legal acts (to which we referred earlier in the text of the present book) are under the purview of national courts of one particular state, which is a state of the corporate nationality.

These are mainly issues within the legal confines of a separate field of law, which is corporate law giving rise to a specific legal phenomenon. That is a corporation as a subject of private law advancing a particular national law idea as to how to represent a state in internal and external relations in order to reach its main end given in constitutional documents.

This competence over proceedings relating to all and any above-mentioned blocks of issues is attributed to national courts notwithstanding domicile, when domicile is the seat of the corporation. And for the purpose of exclusive jurisdiction of UK courts over a list of issues given in national legislation (including uniform international law rules) a corporation has its seat in the UK if and only if it was incorporated or formed under the law of a part of the UK and has its registered office or some other official address in the UK; or its central management and control is exercised in the UK.[131]

This means that the UK assumes jurisdiction over all and any corporations closely or substantially connected with this state through the relevant incorporation procedures within its territory under its laws. And in this connection, should there be any non-compliance with requirements set with respect to exclusive jurisdiction of national courts, judgments made by foreign courts will not take effect and have any force in the United Kingdom.

3.5.1. When foreign corporations are immune from the jurisdiction of foreign national courts

In the present context it is important to admit that immunity is the main property of sovereignty making up an integral attribute of a separate strictly functional and politically independent community extending its power and force over a separate territory within which limits this power is deemed to be supreme. As a general rule, foreign corporations as subjects of private law relations may never be immune from any and all proceedings in respect of personal injuries and damage to property, with no one or nothing excluded from this rule. But there is an exception to this rule. Earlier reference was made to Iraqi legislation granting foreign corporations immunity from jurisdiction in private law cases,[132] but these are exceptional cases. In the private law sphere advancing the idea of formal equality of rights, no immunities may be granted to private law corporations as subjects of cross-border commercial and non-commercial relations.

3.5.2. Prior conditions for foreign judgements to be enforced

For a forum to be deemed appropriate and exercise jurisdiction over a separate private international law dispute in the corporate sphere brought to court, there should be either a close and substantial connection or sufficient connection with the state of the forum, if there is no way to submit this dispute to any other court.

It is necessary to determine this connection with the state of the forum in order to preclude financial losses of the parties when the choice of the forum

---

[131] See Art. 42 of the Civil Jurisdiction and Judgments Act, 1982.

[132] *"Sending States may contract for any services, equipment, provisions, supplies, material, other goods, or construction work to be furnished or undertaken in Iraq without restriction as to choice of supplier or Contractor. Such contracts may be awarded in accordance with the Sending State's laws and regulations. Contractors shall be immune from Iraqi legal process with respect to acts performed by them pursuant to the terms and conditions of a Contract or any sub-contract thereto"* (See Section 4, Para 1 and 3 of Coalition Provisional Authority Order 17.

to the exclusion of all others does not have any effect under procedural rules of the state having a legitimate regulatory interest in a private international law dispute in the corporate sphere. To determine this connection means to employ the very same mechanism resting on subjective and objective criteria as in conflict of law regulation. Among them one may find inextricable link with the home state of issues affecting the state and fate of corporations as well as permanent or stable connection with the place of characteristic performance of contractual obligations, consumer's nationality / domicile / habitual residence; place of employment, business, unjust enrichment, unfair competition as well as all and any obligations in tort.

3.5.3. Recognition of foreign decisions relating to corporate and other rights and obligations arising in this connection

From the general course of theory of law we know that no foreign act may ever take effect outside the territory of the state, which made it without the consent given by the competent authorities to this effect. For details of regulation one may always look at international jurisdiction rules stipulated in national private international law codes or other acts providing for three types of rules (directly applicable, conflict of law rules and international jurisdiction rules) to guide a private law activity closely connected with two or more states in a predictable for public and private law subjects manner.

The following points should be noted:

(1) foreign decisions may not have effect and be considered as final and binding if they are made by inappropriate court. This means that public interest has a dominant role in this issue;

(2) the parties' will to submit their corporate or any other dispute to one particular court to the exclusion of any others based on prorogation and derogation agreements will have distinct legal effect for this court to be considered appropriate if it does not infringe on the public interest of a state closely and substantially connected with private law relations; and

(3) in the absence of the choice there is no other concept to be put forth in the private international law sphere, which could ever displace a concept of close and substantial connection resting on ideas of sovereignty and territoriality of states and their jurisdictions.

In the modern acceptance of this concept, its particulars as well as particulars of its use are laid down in numerous private international law acts of sovereign states. The wording of these rules may differ but the idea remains the same. Recognition of foreign decisions is unavoidable if they respond to the test of close and substantial connection with a private international law dispute. In particular, that is the forum of the state:

– of characteristic performance of contractual obligations;

- of consumer's nationality, domicile or habitual residence under consumer contracts;
- where the work was done under the relevant employment contract;
- where business is placed with respect to operation of the place of business;
- where the act, result took place as to unjust enrichment, unfair competition as well as all and any obligations in tort, to which we referred with respect to particulars of conflict of law regulation.

If the forum does not respond to above-mentioned criteria, no *exequatur* may be given to decisions made by foreign courts in the sphere of private international law of corporations. That is the sphere of social regulation dealing with issues of applicability of distinct legal systems and jurisdiction of national courts over all and any real and good faith controversies arising between the parties of corporate and other relations closely connected with them. These controversies arise in the corporate law sphere over a wide range of private international law issues affecting the legal status of corporations, rights and obligations of their members and other persons involved.

4.   SCALE OF PRIVATE INTERNATIONAL LAW OF CORPORATIONS

There is no common rule-making and rule-enforcing system, because these state functions rest on the idea of sovereignty and territoriality having distinct effects depending on the jurisdiction. Consequently, there is no common measure or test for dealing with the issue as to whether private international law of corporations is a structurally and logically complete legal institute addressing pressing economic, political and social needs and concerns of the time. There is even no common criterion to test and compare legal institutes which are divergent but closely connected for pure practical purposes, composing distinct systems of law in different states.

There are numerous private international law rules set or recognized by sovereign states as necessary to guide law enforcers on separate sets of private law issues according to a number of underlying fundamental principles of natural and positive law. Each set of issues in its part requires a number of its own guiding principles.

With respect to corporations as subjects of a private international law activity, these are the principles deduced from legal theory and practice to be as specific a guide as possible:
(1) unity and integrity of all and any actions affecting the legal status of corporations;
(2) freedom of contract when structuring diverse commercial and non-commercial transactions;
(3) legal paternalism as prevalent in consumer relations.

If this subject is sufficiently determined and completely accords with a law making idea in the relevant sphere of regulation, private international law of corporations is a distinct structurally and logically complete legal institute in the field of law dealing with conflicting regulatory interests of distinct sovereign subjects of law.

On this account, to measure a legal institute means to test for the soundness and utility theories and concepts advanced in the relevant rules of law comprising this legal institute. In other words, this means to show "*ratio legis*" of the relevant legal institute.

The nature of private international law of corporations as a legal institute of the relevant field of law (private international law) has already been discussed, and from this it is clear that nothing in its nature could be treated differently from the nature of other legal institutes of the given field of law in national systems of law. These rules are fashioned both by lawyers and practitioners of law in a manner to bring common satisfaction over settlement of two extremely complicated legal issues by the appropriate means. These are conflicts of laws and conflicts of jurisdictions arising in the private law sphere.

This being so, the ultimate test of a legal institute is stability and efficiency. To test stability and efficiency of the system of private international law of corporations means to consider its guiding principles. These are principles on which this legal institute is founded, enabling it to deal with complicated legal and jurisdictional problems arising in the corporate law sphere. We know that private international law of corporations is a legal institute the primary purpose of which is to give a state and the parties involved the best solution of conflicts of law and forum problems, which they may face when entering into legal relations on a cross-border basis.

In the private international law of corporations for many centuries there was only one idea directing those dealing with territorial extent of laws. That was the idea of a merchant as a subject of private law relations governed in special courts (trade or mercantile courts) by customs, usages and practices of trade falling under the broad category of law of merchants (in Latin – *lex mercatoria*), the oldest phenomenon of the science of social regulation.

Remarkably, the law of merchants is not a system of legal rules of the particular sovereign state, but rather an autonomous system of customs, usages and practices all states agree upon to deal with private law disputes arising in the commercial sphere in a quick and predictable way for the merchants. In other words, it is a system of rulings made by the commercial community to respond to their interests in the well-being on a cross-border basis in the long run.

And what is particularly remarkable in this respect is that in this sphere it is difficult to find something innovative in exercising rights and obligations. Nevertheless, over time specific processes taking place in relevant communities and this passage of time results in:
(1) keeping old ideas alive as they are;
(2) replacing outlived ideas with new ones;
(3) abrading old ideas to respond to new circumstances of the time and place; or
(4) formulating absolutely or relatively new ideas.

Among these new ideas is the legal idea of a foreign corporation as a subject of private international law activity and its role in the growth of national economies. On this account the question arises as to when it was thought convenient to build up a new legal institute inside a system of private international law to deal with legal and jurisdictional problems arising in the private law sphere.

Unlike *lex mercatoria* the principal feature of private international law as a neat way to settle a conflict of law problem, was the idea to keep up private law relations with foreigners or over the property abroad through taking them into special protection of the host state. Under *lex mercatoria* there have always been old ordaining and establishing provisions and procedures to address and determine commercial or trade grievance cases in a simplified manner exerting much influence on merchants' rights and obligations, but not in a way that prioritised cross-border trade.

In retrospect, "merchants" meant all individuals participating in such types of a risk-taking activity as trade and commerce when pursuing some economic or financial end. At this time and for several centuries before there have mainly been companies (corporations) carrying out different types of activity in separate spheres of a socio-economic life of the relevant communities. However, it has always been held that private international law of corporations lives apart from *lex mercatoria* dealing with the same cases but in a peculiar way suggesting different forms of state involvement from giving distinct freedoms in the cross-border corporate activity to providing certain remedies. That is a general rule suffering no exemptions[133] save for the cases, when lex mercatoria becomes an integral part of the relevant system of private international law through incorporation of its provisions into a national legal system.

From the very origin of this legal institute private international law of corporations passed several consequential stages of its sustainable growth anticipated by the relevant circumstances. So, the time came when states decided to unblock barriers to trade and thus make steps necessary to attract foreign investments through sanctioning export and import operations of merchants.

Trade has always been depended on to bring foreign investments to those states, which do not initially possess enough funds to maintain sustainable socio-economic growth and development to the welfare of their people and on that account being under their immediate and direct protection. By way

---

[133] For a more objective view see Art. 7 of the Civil Code of Republic of Armenia, 1998, No. AL-239, in which it is stipulated that *"…a custom of commerce is a rule of conduct in any area of entrepreneurial activity that has taken form and is widely applied, and that is not provided by legislation, regardless of whether or not it has been fixed in any document. Customs of commerce contradicting obligatory provisions of legislation or contract shall not be applied…".*

of illustration, in England starting from the first half of the thirteenth century (Magna Carta or the Great Charter) "all merchants may enter or leave England unharmed and without fear, and may stay or travel within it, by land or water, for purposes of trade, free from all illegal exactions, in accordance with ancient and lawful customs. This, however, does not apply in time of war to merchants from a country that is at war with us. Any such merchants found in our country at the outbreak of war shall be detained without injury to their persons or property, until we or our chief justice have discovered how our own merchants are being treated in the country at war with us. If our own merchants are safe they shall be safe too".

Hence, uthis clause shows the rules-based regime of foreign trade set in England as resting on the idea of mutuality advanced in international relations, foreign merchants could enter English markets, deal freely on them and in case of abuse of rights to obtain redress under territorial laws and customs. And that is not the only legal testament of the time giving rise to private international law relations.

Many centuries after, with development of commercial law in national systems of law of advanced states, one may observe the rise of private international law relations of corporations. As such they have always been vital to national economies offering enormous commercial opportunities to corporations, which phenomenon has already been broadly distributed in different states as the most successful form of collective bargaining. Because, first, a clear and concise meaning was attached to this word in national legislation of developed and developing states; second, this phenomenon was filled with a predictable content for other states for the further recognition of corporate rights and obligations on a cross-border basis.

Hence, it goes back to the eighteenth century and rests on a pure theory of corporations unmixed with a foreign element in its structure but faced with conflicts of law and jurisdiction problems arising from cross-border relations on the purchase or sale, exchange, renting and mortgage of property submitted to law of its situs. That is law of property, law of obligations and other structural elements of domestic law varying depending on the cause and effect of private law relations. At this time one could observe steps made both by jurists and practitioners of law for the construction of a specific way of thinking resting on simple and concise principles (for example, *lex societatis, lex loci, lex voluntatis*) to make known to participants the law and jurisdiction equally applicable to a cross-border activity of corporations in whichever part of the world it could be held.

This stage ends with the enactment of Bustamante Code. That is the Convention on Private International Law made in Havana on 20 February

1928 and addressing all the issues concerned with the legal status of corporations to their personal law by virtue of a conflict of law principle *lex societatis*. It was commonly adopted by a number of early-enacted private international law acts of the second half of the twentieth century, in particular, by the Austrian Act on Private International Law of 1978, by the Hungarian Act on Private International Law of 1979, by the Civil Code of Vietnam 1995. This was the advent of the formation of private international law of corporations.

With the rise of a cross-border commercial activity of corporations the ground was thus prepared for a new stage at which corporations became studied from more standpoints than ever before. This stage brings us to the end of twentieth century and is characterized by the advancement of the theory of corporations as subjects of private international law and development of guiding principles of legal and jurisdictional regulation in terms of well-established contemporary systems of law formulating more precise legal rules to govern complicated corporate law relations and leaving an ever-shrinking area to law enforcers.

As a consequence, a list of corporate and other issues may be found in all newly adopted private international law acts to be resolved by the personal law of corporations. We are now speaking of the stage, which we regard as a transitional one from the rise of a private international law activity of corporations, which greatly facilitated to their regulation in newly adopted private international law acts based on a body of rules specifically formulated by theory and practice of dealing with conflicting regulatory interests of states in the private law sphere, to the stage of legal perfection.

In other words, entering a stage of the formation of the relevant legal institute as a specific systematic arrangement in the structure of private international law, which is deemed to be a great help in maintaining private international law relations through diminishing legal and financial risks of those entering into them, because it sets conditions for the predictable execution of private international law relations, while maintaining the unity and integrity of all and any actions, which affect the legal status of corporations.

Furthermore, if we look at this stage from another angle, ideas of corporate property, possession and succession undergo significant changes to respond to the new socio-economic reality. The culminating point is the tendency to permanent presence of a foreign element in the structure of corporate law forms. This tendency is manifest in the desire to make a corporate activity more international, starting in the 1970s. This tendency takes such forms as foreign incorporators, foreign corporate property as well as a real seat placed abroad etc. These are transnational corporations or if to put it more accurately, a number of companies closely connected with each other through horizontal or vertical ties and managing their activity on a broad cross-territorial basis.

As it may be seen, stages of this legal institute rise and advancement do not coincide with stages characterizing development of private international law as a separate field of law in national systems of law, which origination dates back to the twelfth century AD to special circumstances around the gloss made by Accursius as a silver bullet of the time.[134] Each stage of development of private international law of corporations brought its own notions and terms to crystallize the existing ones. This exercised much influence upon participants of cross-border corporate law relations. But what remained unchanged is the spirit of private international law of corporations, a legal institute dealing with extremely complicated legal and jurisdictional problems arising in the corporate sphere in a manner to maintain unity and integrity of all and any actions affecting the legal status of corporations as subjects of private international law activity. Correspondingly its subject[135] and a method of regulation[136] also remained intact.[137]

---

[134] Accursius is one of the *"founding fathers of private international law"*, to whom we all are deeply indebted for making specific rules for particular circumstances or formulating special guides for the competent authorities of states to lay down new rules found to be acceptable for all nations around the world. These are the circumstances around private law relations burdened with a foreign element(s) (subject or object) tending to its own national public order and entailing conflicting regulatory interests of sovereign states.

[135] These are cross-border corporate and other relations (labour, investment etc.) closely connected with them.

[136] This method of regulation (coordination) of a good many private law cases burdened with a foreign element and consequently submitted to two or more distinct systems of law and jurisdiction rests basically on mandatory rules of national law of corporations of the state closely and substantially connected with them. We say "basically" mainly owing to the fact that in the sphere of private international law regulation of cross-border corporate and other relations closely connected with them each state assigns to individuals a specific area in which their free will may be realized.

[137] This unchangeable unity of specific subject and method of ruling characterize a distinct element of the system. That is a legal institute governing private international law relations arising in a corporate law sphere in a way to ensure harmony in the private law sphere.

Peculiar characteristics of all these stages as well as a general idea of private international law of corporations may be seen in a great number of national law structures and the court practice in distinct sovereign states. They show that the greatest influence upon formation of this legal institute was the aim of individuals with limited domestic opportunities in a commercial sphere to extend them in foreign markets, creating new challenges to collective bargaining.

The main idea underlying collective bargaining is common profit. It is a product of a corporate activity undertaken in a way that also suits these individuals, jointly and conscientiously. This means by the use of specific corporate law forms characterized by a system of limitations adapted to private and/or public law spheres and commonly termed in the legal theory a "legal status of corporations".

This aim received support from sovereign states in the contractual freedom conferred by them through the relevant acts of positive law and as a consequence varying along many lines depending on the time, place and circumstances.

This legal institute, it has obviously long become a separate sphere of ruling inside a system of private international law rules for the extension of the commercial and non-commercial potential of corporations on foreign financial, industrial and other markets. And though it cannot be kept as standing apart from other legal institutes of private international law, it is a distinct structural element of the relevant system resolving legal and jurisdictional conflicts arising in the ruling of cross-border corporate and other relations closely connected with them. That is the scope and boundary determined with necessary exactness by this legal institute, which perfectly serves the end of recognition and protection of private international law rights and obligations of corporations.

4.1. Current state of private international law of corporations

We know that corporate law centres on the idea of a corporation as a subject of law and the power of a distinct sovereign state, be it the state where it carries out its commercial and non-commercial activity or not. The main idea of private international law is the idea of a foreign element appearing as a cause of all and any legal and jurisdictional conflicts to be settled by applicable legal rules and principles. Private international law of corporations as a separate legal institute deals with a peculiar idea. That is the private law idea of a foreign element in the structure of cross-border corporate and other relations closely connected with them.

To discuss this comprehensively and systematically, first, we need to examine the theory and practice of private international law regulation of these relations, and try to answer the following issues: what roles are allotted to theory and practice in this field of law (private international law) and this legal institute (private international law of corporations)? May theory and practice be separated?

These are the points of great importance, because there has always been a common understanding that private international law is law made by practitioners of law and later developed by theorists using appropriate logical methods to give simple and concise rules in order to govern cross-border private law relations in the whole complexity and variability of their combinations.

This means that both practice and theory at all times played an equal role in this particular field of private law. This role becomes apparent from court practice. To be more precise, it becomes apparent from the practice of those dealing with legal and jurisdictional problems on a regular basis and supplies theorists with a necessary legal material. That is the material needed for the refinement of legal reasoning commonly based upon sound argumentation in this sphere of three-fold jurisprudence (public interest, governing law and procedural law).

Experience is useful, but without theory extending and securing it in the right direction, it cannot maintain itself. The same is true of theory, which cannot be practical of itself. In this connection another question arises as to what we may learn and derive from the field of experience? Only experience, aided by philosophy of law, opens up a new path of reasoning. That is the reasoning over numerous legal and jurisdictional problems and patterns to settle them in a way bringing common satisfaction for the good neighbourliness of states, when these problems are burdened with a great number of unpredictable obstacles. The oftener this experience is repeated, the better means we have for the solution of new legal problems we face.

This is because private international law is both practical and theoretical law in that it studies the practice of dealing with problems of conflicts of law and jurisdiction and based on these studies develops new or expands old juristic ideas to handle these problems. These are problems that law enforcers face in each particular case brought to court using certain theoretical instruments and show patterns to settle them. In other words, it seeks answers to all these legal and factual problems confronting those considering the indefinite variety of private law cases.

These are the cases generated by distinct subjective will and resulting in unfamiliar substance. And by this search the sole idea pursued is to give all those charged with the settlement of these problems certain instructions as to how to act when, first, they have to apply to the appropriate forum and choose law applicable to certain legal relations and, second, they have to create, amend, execute or terminate legal rights and obligations with a cross-border effect and thus preclude their disinterest, inability and blindness at the settlement of these problems. For this reason analytical work resting both on theoretical and practical material would be of great help.

This task of law enforcers is extensive and complicated, requiring much effort and skill, because this seeking for a proper resolution of conflicts of law and jurisdiction is accompanied by:

(1) breaking down private law relations into distinct structural elements (subjects and objects);
(2) determination of the origin and role of each of these elements in private law relations;
(3) study and systematization of legal facts around these private international law relations with determinate end, which is to choose law closely connected with these relations based on the relevant practical methods fixed in numerous legal forms.

In this respect it should be noted that these private law relations are characterized by different circumstances instigated by distinct composition and expression of the subjective will.

When focusing upon particulars of these relations it becomes evident that physical and legal persons further their own ends. They differ one from another and sometimes remain absolutely hidden even for the parties with which they enter into legal relations. To reach these distinct ends parties use different means. This also complicates the choice of law and appropriate forum at the settlement of corresponding legal and jurisdictional problems. So, the circumstances of each specific private law case are always unpredictable and difficult.

Returning to the issue of a mutual relation or connection between theory and practice in the issue concerned with the governance of cross-border corporate and other relations closely connected with them, it is apparent that the private international law of corporations encompasses:

(1) distinct practice of settling legal and jurisdictional problems arising in the corporate law sphere in a way predictable for public and private law subjects of the time and place; and
(2) sound theory extending and securing this practice in a peculiar manner.

They are summed up in a way to lay a sound foundation for the practical legal philosophy and philosophical practice of private international law.

The main idea of practical legal philosophy is to put philosophical reasoning of law on special practical grounds satisfying specific rights and interests of both public and private subjects of law. In other words, it is aimed at the transition of theoretical categories of rights and interests into distinct practical means. Law is a pure practical instrument exercising a definite practical effect upon the world and bringing order and harmony in it.

From the review above we know that both theory and practice are equally important in formulating rules and principles to govern specific cross-border corporate law relations and other relations closely connected with them thus offering enormous opportunities in commercial and non-commercial spheres to all those being behind corporations.

The main condition to enter into these relations is recognition by host states of rights conferred by home states. These are both individual and corporate rights ensuring free expression of individual and corporate will in commercial and non-commercial spheres: to do business in whichever form possible and thus exercise general, special or particular powers granted by home states, to own property, to sue and be sued in the appropriate forum etc. These rights are recognized by foreign states through persons dealing with foreign corporations as well as private international law disputes based on the very idea of the common practice set between states and giving rise to the relevant rights and obligations to observe foreign laws enacted in this connection.

This idea has been introduced into law, and is currently held by all advanced jurisdictions in international law incorporated into the national legal system. These are bilateral and multilateral agreements traditionally signed by the rich North and poor South to deal with private law relations burdened with a foreign element. These international law rights and obligations to recognize private law rights and interests of foreigners survive after expiration or renunciation of these international law acts, even if specific procedures are needed, because the world rests on interstate commerce and its developments in distinct socio-economic spheres, which (regardless of multiple tensions) makes it too valuable a benefit both those who sell and those who buy.

Based on this argument, private international law of corporations is law properly so called. It is born of pure practical reasons and includes mandatory and default legal rules, the observance of which is totally necessary in a conflict of rights and legitimate regulatory interests of two or more states in the ruling of private law relations arising between different subjects of law (physical, legal persons and even states acting in a non-sovereign quality) in the corporate law sphere. It has a specific intrinsic mechanism guiding law enforcers and other persons charged with the ruling of corporate actions in a predictable manner for sovereign persons. Hence, this law is imperative, as is the law of corporations with which private international law of corporations is closely and essentially connected.

By determining the imperative nature and essence of private international law of corporations, it should be acknowledged that lawmakers attribute a specific value to this legal institute in the system of private law. Corporations as permanent participants of commercial and non-commercial legal relations with cross-border impact deserve special attention. These are persons fit for the settlement of multiple private and public law issues and assigned with a relevant scope of rights and duties to meet multifarious needs.

The reasons to base this conclusion on are:

(1) **nature of ruling** – private international law of corporations is practical law addressing a good number of complicated issues arising in a private international law sphere;

(2) **character of ruling** – private international law of corporations is mandatory law suggesting commands and judgments in the settlement of numerous cross-border corporate and other disputes brought to court;

(3) **subject matter of specific practical and mandatory ruling** – private international law of corporations is a body of directly applicable, conflict of law rules and rules on international jurisdiction to govern cross-border corporate law relations and other relations closely connected with them in a way to reconcile conflicting interests of two or more states over their regulation.

In line with other legal institutes private international law of corporations is subjected to continuous refinement to respond to current socio-economic concerns of communities with which we will deal in the next, final part of this book.

4.2. Prospects and problems of modern private international law of corporations

There is one interesting observation on corporation: even though it is not a recent development, it is one of the greatest privileges once granted by states to persons, being in state of subjection to them, one of the most important effects of which is the extension of private law rights and interests to help individuals to navigate choppy waters of interstate trade and commerce. The reason is that corporations are privileged to do things, which individuals may not do in their initial quality of subjects of civil law.

However, corporations serve not only private law rights and interests but also interests of sovereign states (home and host states). At the current stage of socio-economic development of states, corporations are very powerful instrument in their hands, conferred with an exceedingly complex aggregate of legal rights, obligations and responsibility. They may be used in response to various pressing needs and concerns faced by states in political, economic and social spheres. On this there is universal agreement. Moreover, being a product of the time and place and later assumed as a rational one, corporations may steadily grow for many more years and at the same time respond to challenges, which may lie ahead without losing their particular utility for national economies.

For example, look at the scope and intensity of recent developments in the sphere of corporate law. It is evident that the structure of corporations (as well as a structure of corporate property) underwent serious changes granting many opportunities to those, whose names are subscribed to a memorandum of a private law association or any other act prescribed by national law of a corporation as a constitutional act, and to other persons concerned (beneficiaries etc.). Taking into consideration the number and value of all these developments, there is hardly any other private law sphere characterized by such a rapid development.

But when resting on such a solid foundation as the theory of certitude in the nature and essence of corporate law relations, these changes may never be considered as critical and requiring a new legal framework. This framework rests on one of the greatest juridical ideas. That is the unchangeable idea of a corporation as a form of a voluntary association of individuals characterized by the limited liability and shared property, to which a home state concedes (and host states recognize) a separate legal capacity to exercise its free will over things and actions to make profit or attain any other legally enforceable common end (objective) under a separate name. And what is true of the unchangeable nature and essence of corporate law is evidently true of its unchallengeable spirit reflected in the persistent course of dealing with individual freedom in commercial and non-commercial spheres in a way meeting public law interests.

Specific properties of corporations distinguishing them from other legal forms determined to advance national economies, and it is evident that they contribute much to positive ideas of:

(1) sanctity of private property, to which particular importance has always been given;

(2) sanctity of labour and acknowledgement of its particular role in origination and maintenance of property relations;[138] and

(3) limited liability of those involved in a joint commercial and non-commercial activity.

Making up the general idea of a corporation these private law ideas have always been sufficiently uniform notwithstanding the place of their operation to make corporations the main drivers of national economies. For this reason, in general there is not much difference between them except for details into which states enter peculiarly in accordance with distinct interests of the peoples they represent. These are those appearing from peculiar views on different things and resulting in special legal theories of corporations framed by states to underlie multifarious legal forms when implementing the idea of the national corporate law mechanism.

Throughout history, different functions have always been allotted to corporations from those relating to a social sphere to purely commercial. From the time of the Roman Empire corporations played a significant role in both private and public law spheres. And probably they were simply fated to survive in any circumstances. No economy can exist without national and foreign direct and indirect investments of corporations, taxes and other duties paid by them to national budgets.

Their actual tasks gradually grow and extend. But this should not entail subsequent transformation of corporations into new forms of associations with absolute power in order to be above individuals and thus be out of state control. We must never forget the initial idea of a corporation being to let individuals be free.[139] However this should never be taken as an absolute freedom. Because the history shows us too many misfortunes resulting from total deregulation by sovereign states over their members. So, it seems to be

---

[138] For evidence of this consider the general principles of economic activity in Brazil. Under Art. 170 of BC 1988 *"the economic order, founded on the appreciation of the value of human labor and free enterprise, is intended to assure everyone a dignified existence, according to the dictates of social justice, observing the following principles: I. national sovereignty; II. private property; III. social function of property; IV. free competition; V. consumer protection; VI. environmental protection, including through differentiated treatment in accordance with the environmental impact of the products and services and the processes by which they are elaborated and rendered; VII. reduction in regional and social inequalities; VIII. pursuit of full employment; IX. preferential treatment for small-scale firms organized under Brazilian law with their headquarters and management in the Country"*.

[139] The main principle in accordance with which they exist is the corporate freedom as the individual freedom of those voluntary entering into a joint commercial and non-commercial activity.

evident that if there is no power above no one may thrive, for the absolute freedom and absolute disaster are synonymous.

A person and a state as two parties taken abstractedly are closely connected with each other. The two of them are free within defined limits. But it is understood that when they pursue their aims under the influence of particular financial interests this should not run counter legal interests of the opposite side of private law relations. Besides there are situations when, to prevent the true freedom from being interfered, the best way to preserve it is to constrain it in some part meeting the main end.

That is a system of limitations developed in detail both by jurists and practitioners of law and establishing certain limits of what is right and wrong for a corporation as a particular subject of law. It is specifically tailored for each community and takes its unique form at the very formation of a corporation for the latter to act lawfully, to prevent misuse of rights, to give employees, creditors, and incorporators their due and thus further public interest of the relevant community.

In practice, an ever-shrinking area of freedom has been left to corporations. They must act strictly within permitted limits to a defined purpose so as to meet public interest requirements of home states. In the private international law sphere this freedom rests on the choice of law and forum in cross-border commercial and non-commercial relations of the parties with comparable bargaining power forging predictable effect of private international law regulation.

Corporate law produces a corporation as a legal form of a voluntary association of individuals to pursue one common idea to give them a chance to extend their potential in commercial and non-commercial spheres. In private international law we usually label this "financial (economic) interest" enacted under national law. Also, corporate law supplies a firm and sound basis to advance corporate law relations inside a definite community, and produces the most suitable concepts for enacting by states and their members. One such is the concept of personal liability of members of corporations instructing their management in a manner to act contrary to national laws and contractual/extra contractual duties these corporations entered into.

Private international law of corporations expands the area of their commercial and non-commercial activity through recognition by host states of the corporate personality once given in all its variety by a home state striving to give individuals the best form, which they ever may frame. It therefore becomes apparent that in special circumstances corporate law cannot be considered as complete and sufficient in itself in the regulation of corporate and other issues closely connected with them on a cross-border basis. Private international law of corporations maintains corporate law, and its further sustainable development in a predictable way for public and private law interests.

The main aim of private international law of corporations is unerring choice of law and jurisdiction to cross-border corporate relations and other relations closely connected with them based on peculiar legal principles produced by legal theory and practice with due regard to a specific nature and constitution of corporations. This aim correlates with the aim of corporate law itself guiding the conduct of the parties under an obligation in a specific sphere of a socio-economic activity and showing the means to attain the end of this conduct. Therefore as soon as legal rules governing corporate law relations cannot be disregarded, likewise, the law ruling cross-border corporate relations and other relations closely connected with them will not lose its efficiency. And this makes private international law of corporations particularly attractive for jurists and practitioners of law globally.

Rapidly changing economic circumstances and general uncertainty in economic and other markets of late generated by the intensive use of new technologies exert much influence on the social function of corporations. This may be viewed as a compelling force for the further economic growth of national economies under these new circumstances.

Using new technologies corporations may give individuals advanced solutions in retail. These are autonomous staffless mobile stores turning every parking space in the world into a potential new 24-hour store.[140] However, we are also well aware of what they do not give them to improve their social state though they could.

For example, corporations do not give economic and social security to those who do not directly deal with them on the basis of comparable bargaining power. These are individuals in danger of unemployment as of corporations benefit from the use of staffless stores, plants etc. in the workplace.

No one ever raised this issue in the private international law doctrine and practice but it definitely deserves attention, because economic capability is one of the pillars of sovereignty in line with security capability and territorial integrity. On that account, it is time to think of future generations, who will enjoy the benefit of our care, if we just start caring about them now.

---

[140] See the site of the Moby Mart: www.themobymart.com

And if we care now about social security and social health of distinct communities we will not face these arduous issues in future.

While corporations are ideal instruments to advance prosperity of relevant communities and protect their gradual growth in the long run. It is not an easy task to predict new challenges that corporations may meet to ensure the freedom of individuals in commercial and non-commercial spheres. We know corporations as a veil for those who own them but this should not be the only assignment. Lawmakers must increase their social accountability through extension of the following legal categories "solidarity", "responsibility" and "guarantees" in the corporate law sphere.

These are not randomly given legal categories. With varying intensity they evidence a specific legal nature and a particular social role of corporations and perfectly ensure and maintain very sensitive for the relevant communities corporate law obligations. New socially responsible corporate law forms and institutions founded upon these extended legal categories are vital for modern interstate commerce to respond to longer term socio-economic trends and demands in interests of all communities. This will ensure our firm adherence to the theory of corporations to produce functionally different corporate law forms for many years to come.

Neither corporate law nor private international law of corporations as emanations of the common legal reasoning can explain why the corporation, this unique legal phenomenon, was produced, what was the cause of its strong support and development. However, they give us an answer to the question what to do in order to have this phenomenon properly used in private and public law spheres in the long run.

Based on this, corporate law can be expected to thrive as law covering an association of persons pursuing one common end with a bundle of rights and duties under the relevant contract. We can expect the subsequent extension of private international law of corporations as law recognizing this association of persons as a separate subject of private international law and a subject of private international law relations and ensuring the growth of the cross-border corporate activity, because there is scope for much more development of these two fields of private law specifically drafted for those dealing with commercial and non-commercial private law issues jointly. Finally, corporations will never operate free from the power of states, in which they were set up to pursue a very important for private and public law subjects end.

5. CONCLUSION

The private international law of corporations has public interest and interests of justice as focal points of socio-economic ruling in a legal world split into numerous territorial systems of law and jurisdictions. Being distinct legal ideas, these interests underlie such a class of social rules which as rules of law, ensure harmonious social living in any community and enable it to grow and prosper under particular circumstances. They are also present in a separate type of rules of law. These are corporate law rules standing for sustainable socio-economic growth of communities through granting opportunities to those pursuing common financial or economic goals in separate socio-economic spheres.

As far as individual freedom is concerned, there are private international law rules (directly applicable material law rules, conflict of law rules and rules on international jurisdiction) dealing with a concurrence of fundamental sovereign rights of states, which may be observed when a foreign element is present in legal relations which individuals enter into singly or jointly with others.

In the corporate sphere these rules protect rights and interests of those entering into cross-border corporate relations and other relations closely connected with them and facing legal and jurisdictional problems arising in the course of the interstate commercial and non-commercial activity of corporations. They do so in a way to ensure public interest and interests of justice. Private international law can be ascribed an intermediate position between substantive law, law of justice and procedural law in national systems of law.

Cross-border corporate law development require a structurally and logically complete legal institute in the system of private international law rules to deal with complicated legal and jurisdictional issues of interstate trade and commerce. This issue is handled by legal systems. We have a body of rules in national private international law acts governing cross-border corporate relations and other relations closely connected with them in a systematic manner.

This does not entail more favourable trading conditions; that is the end of other social instruments. However, private international law is something both private and public law subjects cannot do without. It is the only field of law to encourage commercial and non-commercial transactions of individuals acting singly or jointly with others by removing as many severe legal and jurisdictional problems which may arise when a distinct public (national/foreign) policy underlies the conduct of private law subjects.

To deal with them it employs strong legal means neatly fixed in numerous national private international law acts to make individuals challenge their limits from the cross-border use of property and labour and try to their maximum benefit from them secured by national and foreign law. Within the corporate sphere, structuring commercial and non-commercial deals of individuals acting jointly when pursuing one common economic (financial) interest, these are rules ensuring unity and integrity of corporations.

These are directly applicable material law rules, conflict of law rules and rules on international jurisdiction dealing with legal and jurisdictional problems related to extension of (1) functionality of corporations through providing goods and services abroad or (2) their composition generating conflicting legitimate regulatory interests of sovereign states, with which these services, activities and foreign direct and indirect investments are closely connected.

In this particular sphere of regulation the main role is allotted to *lex societatis*. That is a conflict of law principle, the importance of which is unquestionable for the position it takes is a result of:

(1) proper reflection of the nature of corporateness;
(2) determination with certainty of law applicable to relations on formation, reorganization, insolvency and termination of corporations so as to ensure unity of all and any corporate actions affecting the status of corporations; and
(3) certain practical reasons underlying this choice to the exclusion of any other connection than the single connection with a home state of a corporation with respect to the effect of this law operation.

The main merits of this legal institute have been demonstrated, showing what it was, is and ought to be when viewed through institutional, scientific, practical, strategic and economic dimensions rather than mere illustrating what we believe it to be. Private international law of corporations is a structurally and logically complete legal institute of private international law addressing pressing economic, political, social and strategic needs of the relevant community through removing legal and jurisdictional obstacles of the most serious nature in the corporate law sphere by the use of distinct legal principles grounded upon ideas of fraternity and reciprocity.

For the extension of the commercial and non-commercial potential of corporations on foreign industrial, financial and other markets it has long become a separate sphere of ruling inside a relevant system of private international law rules. And though it cannot be viewed in isolation from other legal institutes of private international law, it is a distinct structural element of the relevant system characterized by a specific subject, method, problems and perspectives providing a firm basis for the subsequent specific development.

This legal institute embodies the story of corporate law development, which extends to other systems of law through advancing interstate trade and commerce. Knowledge of the distinguishing marks and points of private international law of corporations extends our understanding of corporate law. That is law, which produced a corporation as a separate legal phenomenon which is extremely valuable in both practical and theoretical senses.

This knowledge also extends our understanding of private international law of corporations. That is a distinct legal institute in the system of private international law, the operation of which rests on a number of principles to ensure:

(1) unity and integrity of all and any corporate law actions affecting the legal status of corporations;

(2) freedom of contract when structuring diverse commercial and non-commercial transactions; and

(3) legal paternalism as prevalent in consumer relations corporations enter into.

These principles are deduced from legal theory and practice to govern a specific subject matter as completely as possible through (1) removing legal and jurisdictional problems arising in real and good faith actions affecting the legal status of corporations, title to property and other rights of corporations and other persons concerned on a cross-border basis and (2) developing corporate law as well as specific national law concepts and principles underlying private international law.

This is the root of my opinion that private international law of corporations is a separate structurally complete legal institute of private international law embracing directly applicable rules, conflict of law rules and international jurisdiction rules governing cross-border corporate and other legal relations closely connected with them.

CONCLUSION

Glossary

Applicable (governing) law is material law of the state closely and substantially related with a private law relation burdened with a foreign element (subject or object) tending to a separate national public order.

Appropriate jurisdiction is the power of the court anchored in the national legal system to hear and determine a private law case burdened with a foreign element.

Conflict of laws is a collision of legitimate regulatory interests of two or more states in the ruling of private law relations arising between different subjects of law (physical, legal persons and even states acting in a non-sovereign capacity), which for the reason of significant controversy in their implementation place them in the hands of judges to assert private law rights and obligations.

Conflict of law rules are legal rules for delimitation of legitimate regulatory interests of different states in private law relations closely connected with more than one state in a predictable for these states manner.

Conflict of law method of private international law of corporations is a necessary process in the choice of proper law to corporate and other relations closely connected with them, by which law enforcers take definite steps relying on concrete conditions of each private law case placed in their hands to assert and establish private law rights and obligations to the ideal, which is unity and integrity of corporations.

Corporate nationality is more than a mere corporate location of business, it is loyalty and commitment of those constituting a corporation to a particular state conferring them with a distinct number of legal rights, duties and responsibility in order to deal freely in commercial and non-commercial spheres of a socio-economic life of the relevant community as one party independent of them.

Corporate property is a complex of material and non-material things (including intellectual property rights) exclusively held by a corporation, to which they were given by individuals acting singly or jointly with others to further one common end or acquired by a corporation at its distinct from individuals corporate life.

Corporation is a form of a voluntary association of individuals characterized by limited liability and shared property, to which a home state concedes (and host states recognize) a separate legal capacity to exercise its free will over things and actions to make a profit or attain any other legally enforceable common end (objective) under a separate name.

Corporate rights are rights of individuals to contract a specific legal status giving certain immunities to incorporators against debts and other obligations taken by corporations.

Foreign corporation is a form of a voluntary association of individuals having all attributes, rights, benefits, privileges and immunities as they are ascribed to corporations by foreign laws and recognized and maintained by national laws.

Foreign law is a separate system of law of a foreign sovereign state, the contents of which should be established by the court at trial for the purpose of the settlement of all and any legal problems arising in private international law disputes.

Jurisdiction is the extent of the sovereign power to make legal decisions and/or judgments on all and any issues arising in both private and public law spheres with a broad extra-territorial effect.

Immunity is the main property of sovereignty making up an integral attribute of a separate strictly functional and politically independent community extending its power and force over a separate territory within which this power and force are deemed to be supreme.

Law of merchants (or in Latin – *lex mercatoria*) is a system of customs, usages and practices, all states agree upon to deal with any private law disputes arising in the commercial sphere in a way to ensure expediency and predictability for merchants.

Legal institute is a system of legal rules dealing with a particular type of private law relations and forming an integral part of a particular field of law.

Legal personality is a form of manifestation of distinct private law rights and obligations conferred (imposed) by a home state to a voluntary association of individuals characterized by limited liability and shared property to exercise its free will over things and actions to make profit or attain any other legally enforceable common end (objective) inside a separate community or on a cross-border basis under a separate name.

Legal relation is voluntary or involuntary exchange of legal rights and obligations in the private law sphere and characterized by formal equality, autonomy of will and property independence of those entering into them ensured and maintained by sovereign states.

National law of a corporation is the law of a state in which public/ trade/ commercial register this corporation is entered in the quality of a subject of law.

Private international law dispute is a matter of a real and significant controversy between the parties to a contract or arising beyond the bounds of a contract over private law rights and obligations (their cause, particulars of the use and effect) submitted to two or more separate legal orders for a foreign element present in such contractual and extra contractual relations of the parties.

Private international law is a solid, durable and practical system composed of specific legal rules and principles worked out using different languages but in a manner converging public interests of different states at one point for their common application to the endless variety of private law cases burdened with irregular blending of foreign elements tending to different national public orders.

Private international law dispute is a matter of real, significant and good faith controversy between the parties to a contract or arising beyond the bounds of a contract over private law rights and obligations (their cause, particulars of the use and effect) submitted to two or more distinct national legal orders.

Private international law of corporations is a structurally and logically complete legal institute of private international law addressing pressing economic, political, social and strategic needs of the relevant community through governance of cross-border corporate relations and other relations closely connected with them by distinct legal principles functioning based on interests of fraternity and reciprocity.

Private international law relations are legal relations as they are found to be established on a cross-border basis between definite persons (corporations, individuals and states) by their deliberate (voluntary) or undeliberate (involuntary) actions (contractual and extra contractual relations) as the case may be.

Public interest is a specific sovereign idea through keeping away from what is not amenable to a nature of a particular community, making it grow and prosper under particular circumstances.

Science of private international law is certain and evident knowledge of means to settle conflict of law problems arising in a private law sphere around the world for the reason of a foreign element present in the structure of commercial and non-commercial private law relations.

Sovereignty (a general notion) is an integral attribute of a separate strictly functional and politically independent community extending its power and force over a separate territory within which this power is deemed to be supreme.

State is a strictly functional and politically independent community, characterized by the supreme power in internal relations as well as sovereignty, freedom, independence and equality in external relations with other sovereign and non-sovereign communities known to international law.

Bibliography

Armour, John, and Ringe, Wolf-Georg. 2010. "European Company Law 1999 – 2010: Renaissance and Crisis," Oxford Legal Studies Research Paper No. 64/2010.

Austin, John, 1869. "Lectures on Jurisprudence of the Philosophy of Positive Law," London.

Bandyopadhyay, Pramathanath. 1920. "International law and custom in Ancient India," Calcutta University Press.

Bar, L.v. 1892. "The Theory and Practice of Private International Law," William Green & Sons Law Publishers. Edinburgh.

Bastiat, Frédéric. 1850. "La Loi," Librairie de Guillaumin Et Cet, Paris.

Baty, T. 1914. "Polarized Law. Three Lectures on Conflicts of Law," Stevens and Haynes. London.

Black, Bernard S. 1990. ''Is Corporate Law Trivial? A Political And Economic Analysis,'' 84 Northwestern University Law Review 542–97.

Braendle, Udo C., and Noll, Juergen. 2005. "The Societas Europaea – A Step Towards Convergence of Corporate Governance Systems?", Department for Business Administration, University of Vienna.

Beale, Joseph Henry. 1916. "A treatise on the Conflict of Laws of Private International Law," Harvard University Press, Cambridge. Vol. 1. Part. 1

Bingham, Lord. 2010. "Widening Horizons – the influence of comparative law and international law on domestic law," The Hamlyn Lectures.

Bryce, James. "Studies in History and Jurisprudence," Oxford University Press, New York. Vol. II.

Bohoslavsky, Juan Pablo and Opgenhaffen, Veerle. 2010. "The Past and Present of Corporate Complicity: Financing the Argentinean Dictatorship," Harvard Human Rights Journal. Vol. 23.

Born, Gary B. 1992. "A Reappraisal of the Extraterritorial Reach of U.S. Law," 24 Law & Pol'y Int'l Bus. 1.

Calamita, N.Jansen. 2006. "Rethinking Comity: Towards a Coherent Treatment of International Parallel Proceedings," U. Pa. J. Int'l Econ. L. Vol. 27:3.

Carrington, Paul D.. 1989. "Substance" and "Procedure" in the Rules Enabling Act," Duke Law Journal. Volume 1989. Number 2.

Cutler, A. Claire. 2002. Private International Regimes and Interfirm Cooperation. In The Emergence of Private Authority in Global Governance, edited by Rodney Bruce Hall, and Thomas J. Biersteker, 23-40. Cambridge: Cambridge University Press.

Childress, Donald Earl III. 2010. "Comity as Conflict: Resituating International Comity as Conflict of Laws," University of California, Davis. Vol. 44:011.

Childress, Donald Earl III. 2011. "When Erie Goes International," Northwestern University Law Review. 105:1531.

Cohen, Julius. 1961. "Judicial "Legisputation" and the Dimensions of Legislative Meaning," Indiana Law Journal.

Dammann, Jens, and Hansmann, Henry. 2005. "Extraterritorial Courts for Corporate Law," ECGI-Law Working Paper 43/2005.

Davies, Llewelyn. 1937. "The Influence of Huber's De Conflictu Legum on English Private International Law," British Yearbook of International Law. Vol. 18.

Davis, John P. 1905. "Corporations," The Knickerbocker Press.

Easterbrook, Frank H., and Daniel R. Fischel. 1989. "The Corporate Contract," 89 Columbia Law Review 1416–48.

Ehrenzweig, Albert A. 1961. "Choice of Law: Current Doctrine and True Rules," California Law Review. Vol. 49. Issue 2.

Enriques, Luca. 2005. "Company Law Harmonization Reconsidered: What Role for the EC?", EGGI – Law Working Paper No. 53/2005.

Fletcher, George P. 1985. "Paradoxes in Legal Thought," Columbia Law Review. Vol. 85:1263.

Fowler V.Harper. 1959. "Torts, Contracts, Property, Status, Characterization, and the Conflict of Laws," Columbia Law Review. Vol. 59.

Frederick the Great. 1758. "Royal Dissertations on Manners, Customs, etc.," Mecaenas, Dublin.

Freund, Ernst. 2000. "The Legal Nature of Corporations," Batoche Books, Canada.

Gordon, Jeffrey. 1989. "The Mandatory Structure of Corporate Law," 89 Columbia Law Review 1549–98.

Gotzmann, Nora, Legal Personality of the Corporation and International Criminal Law: Globalisation, Corporate Human Rights Abuses and the Rome Statute (2008) Queensland Law Student Review.

Griffith, Sean J.. 2005. "Good Faith Business Judgment: A Theory of Rhetoric in Corporate Law Jurisprudence," 55 Duke L. J. 1 (2005-2006).

Guzman, Andrew T. 2001. "Choice of Law: New Foundations," The Georgetown Law Journal. Vol. 90:883.

Hadfield, Gillian, and Talley, Eric. 2004. "On Public versus Private Provision of Corporate Law." University of South Carolina Law and Economics Research Paper 04–18.

Hamilton, Sir William. 1873. "Philosophy," D.Appleton and Company, New York.

Hansmann, Henry, and Kraakman, Reinier. 2000. "The Essential Role of Organizational Law," 110 Yale Law Journal.

Hansmann, Henry, and Kraakman, Reinier, and Squire, Richard. 2005. "The New Business Entities in Evolutionary Perspective," 2005 Illinois Law Review 5–14.

Hansmann, Henry 2006. "Corporation and Contract," Yale Law School and ECGI. 66/2006.

Hopt, Klaus J. 2005. "European Company Law and Corporate Governance: Where Does the Action Plan of the European Commission Lead?", Oxford University Press.

Hopt, Klaus J. 2006. "Comparative Company Law," Oxford University Press.

Jackman, William J. 1915. "Corporations Organization, Finance and Management," Washington Institute. Chicago.

Joerges, Christian. 2003. "The Challenges of Europeanization in the Realm of Private Law: A Plea for a New Legal Discipline," Duke Journal of Comparative & International Law. Vol. 14:149.

Josephus Jitta. 1907. "La Substance Des Obligations Dans Le Droit International Privé," Librairie Belinfante Frères, la Haye.

Juenger, Frederich. 1983. "General Course on Private International Law".

Kant, Immanuel. 1795. "Perpetual Peace," London.

Kant, Immanuel. 1887. "The Philosophy of Law. An Exposition of the Fundamental Principles of Jurisprudence as the Science of Right," T. & T. Clark, 38 George Street, Edinburgh.

Klausner, Michael. 1995. "Corporations, Corporate Law and Networks of Contracts," 81 Virginia Law Review.

Kramer, Larry. 1990. "Rethinking Choice of Law," 90 COLUM. L. REV. 277.

Kramer, Larry. 1991. "More Notes on Methods and Objectives in the Conflict of Laws," 24 CORNELL INT'L L.J.

Kuhn, Thomas S. 1962. "The Structure of Scientific Revolutions," The University of Chicago Press, Chicago. Vol. II.

Laine A. 1905. "La redaction du Code civil et le droit international prive," Revue de droit international prive. V. 1

Legrand, Pierre. 1997. "Against a European Civil Code," The Modern Law Review. Vol. 60. No. 1.

Leoni, Bruno. 1961. "Freedom and the Law," D Van Nostrand Company, Inc. Princeton, New Jersey.

Lorenzen, Ernest G. 1930. "Pan-American Code of Private International Law," Tulane Law Review.

Lorenzen, Ernest G. 1920. "Theory of Qualifications and the Conflict of Laws," Columbia Law Review. Vol. XX. No. 3.

Lorenzen, Ernest G. 1934. "Story's Commentaries on the Conflict of Laws – One Hundred Years After," Harvard Law Review. Vol. 48.

Lucretius. 1910. "On the nature of things," Clarendon Press. Oxford.

Macdonald, Duncan B. 1903. "Development of Muslim Theology, Jurisprudence and Constitutional Theory," Charles Scribner's Sons, New York.

Maier, Harold G. 1982. "Extraterritorial Jurisdiction at a Crossroads: An Intersection Between Public and Private International Law," 76 AM. J. INT'L L.

Massé, M.G.. 1874. "Le Droit Commercial Dans Ses Rapports Avec Le Droit Des Gens Et Le Droit Civil," Gullaumin Et Cie, Libraires, Paris.

McClintock, H.L. 1930. "Distinguishing Substance and Procedure in the Conflict of Laws," University of Pennsylvania Law Review. Vol. 78

Mill, John Stuart. 1878. "Political Economy with some of their applications to social philosophy," Longmans, London.

Milton Vernon Lyndes. 1949. "The Concept of The Public Interest. Thesis," Boston University School of Public Relations.

Mitchell, W. 1904. "An Essay on the Early History of the Law Merchant," University Press. Cambridge.

Moyle, J.B. trans. 1911. "Justinian, Institutes," Oxford.

Orts, Eric W. 1993. "The Complexity and Legitimacy of Corporate Law," Washington and Lee Law Review. Vol.50:1565.

Pascal, Robert A.. 1940. "Characterization as an Approach to the Conflict of Laws," Louisiana Law Review. Vol. 2, Number 4.

Pasotti, Piero and Lombardo, Stefano. 2004. "The "Societas Europaea": A Network Economics Approach," EGGI – Law Working Paper No. 19/2004.

Paul, Joel R. 1991. "Comity in International Law," Harvard International Law Journal. Vol. 1, 4

Pollock, Frederick. 1912. "The Genius of the Common Law," The Columbia University Press.

Popkin, William D. 1993. "Law-Making Responsibility and Statutory Interpretation," Indiana Law Journal.

Pothier, M. 1806. "A Treatise on the Law of Obligations or Contracts," London, Vol. 2.

Prebble, John. 1973. "Choice of Law to Determine the Validity and Effect of Contracts: A Comparison of English and American Approaches to the Conflict of Laws," Cornell Law Review. Vol. 58, Number 4.

Re, Edward D. 1961. "The Roman Contribution to the Common Law," Fordham Law Review. Vol. 29. Issue 3.

Ruggie, John Gerard. 1993. "Territoriality and Beyond: Problematizing Modernity in International Relations," International Organization. Vol. 47. No. 1.

Salah, M. Mahmoud Mohamed. 2010. "Droit Economique et Droit International Privé".

Scherer, Andreas Georg, Guido Palazzo, and Dorothee Baumann. 2006. Global Rules and New Private Actors: Toward A New Role of the

Transnational Corporation in Global Governance. Business Ethics Quarterly 16 (4):505-32.

Schwartz, Alan and Robert. 2003. "Contract Theory and the Limits of Contract Law," Yale Law Journal, Vol. 113.

de Secondat, Charles Louis, Baron de Montesquieu. 1748. The Spirit of Laws. Complete Works, London, printed for T. Evans, in the Strand; and W.Davis in Piccadilly, Vol. 1.

Shaunnagh, Dorsett and McVeigh, Shaun. 2007. "The Persona of the Jurist in Salmond's Jurisprudence: On the Exposition of "What Law Is...," 38 VUWLER.

Spiro, Peter J. 1996. "New Global Potentates: Nongovernmental Organizations and the "Unregulated" Market Place," Cardzo Law Review 18:957-69.

Stone, Harlan F. 1915. "Law and Its Administration," Columbia University Press, New York.

Story J. 1834. "Commentaries on the Conflict of Laws, Foreign and Domestic," Boston.

Sullivan, John J. 1910. "American Corporations," D. Appleton and Company, New York.

Sumner Maine, Henry. 1883. "Dissertations on Early Law and Custom," Henry Holt and Company, New York.

Symeonides, Symeon C.. 2013. "Codifying Choice of Law Around the World," Oxford University Press.

Taintor, Charles W. II. 1939. "Universality" in the Conflict of Laws of Contracts," Louisiana Law Review. Vol. 1, Number 1.

Tallman, Stephen B., and Yip, George S. 2003. Strategy and the Multinational Enterprise In The Oxford Handbook of International Business, edited by Rugman, Alan M. and Brewer, Thomas 317-48. Oxford: Oxford University Press.

Thring, Lord. 1902. "Practical Legislation. "The Composition And Language of Acts of Parliament And Business Documents," London John Murray, Albemarle Street.

Wharton F. 1905. "A Treatise on the Conflict of Laws or Private International Law," Boston.

White, James J.. 1991. "Ex Proprio Vigore," Michigan Law Review. Vol. 89:2096.

Works, John D. 1894. "Courts and their jurisdiction," The Robert Clarke Company, Cincinnati.

Wymeersch, Eddy. 1999. The Centros: A Landmark Decision in European Company Law," Financial Law Institute Working Paper 99-15.

Wymeersch, Eddy. 2003. "The Transfer of the Company's Seat in European Company Law," EGGI Working Paper Series in Law. No. 08/2003.

Ypi, Lea. 2010. "A Permissive Theory of Territorial Rights," CSSJ Working Papers Series SJ014.

Table of cases

Club Resorts Ltd. v. Van Breda [2012] 1 SCR 572 at para 15 [ABA Tab 16].

Cox v Ministry of Justice [2016] UKSC.

Ministry of Defence v Iraqi Civilians [2016] UKSC 25.

Kennedy v Charity Commissioners [2014] UKSC 20, [2015] AC 455

Mr A M Mohamud (in substitution for Mr A Mohamud (deceased)) v WM Morrison Suprermarkets plc [2016] UKSC 11.

Pinney v.Nelson, 22 Sup. Court Rep. (U. S.) 52 (1901).

Woodland v Swimming Teachers Association [2012] UKSC 66; [2014] AC 537.

Table of statutes

Bill S. 1876, introduced in the Senate of the United States on 14 May 1971.

Brazil's Constitution of 1988 with amendments through 2014.

Civil and Criminal Procedure Code of Bhutan, 2001.

Civil Code of Republic of Armenia, July 28, 1998 AL-239.

Civil Code of the Russian Federation, 1994.

Civil Jurisdiction and Judgments Act, 1982.

Coalition Provisional Authority Order 17.

Companies Act of Belize, 2003.

Companies Act of the Bahamas, 1992.

Companies Act of Botswana, 2007.

Constitution de la Principauté, 1962.

Constitution of the Republic of Malawi, 1994.

STATUTES

Constitution of the Republic of Serbia, 2006

Consumer Rights Act, 2015.

Foreign Limitation Periods Act, 1984.

French Civil Code, 2013, No. 2013-404.

French Consumer Code, 2005, No. 2005-1086.

Hague Convention on the Law Applicable to Trusts and on their Recognition, 1985.

Law of Ukraine on Private International Law, 2005 No. 2709-IV.

Law on Private International Law of the Czech Republic, No. 91/2012.

Riforma del sistema italiano di diritto internazionale private, 1995, n. 218

Polish Act on Private International Law, 2011.

Private International Law (Miscellaneous Provisions) Act, 1995.

Private International Law Code of the Republic of Tunisia, 1998.

Proclamation of Independence, 1948.

Protection Against Unfair Competition Act, 2000, No. 589.

Regulation (EC) of the European Parliament and of the Council on the law applicable to contractual obligations (Rome I), 2008, No 593/2008.

Spanish Civil Code, 2009.

State Immunity Act, 1978.

Swiss Federal Act on Private International Law, 2014.

Turkish Act on Private International and Procedural Law, 2007, No. 5718.

Index

Accursius....................................... 130

appropriate forum ....
.... 8, 13, 34, 115, 133

Armenia
Civil Code 66, 127, 155

Austria....................................... 129

Bahamas 76

Belarus.. 4

Belize.................................... 16, 155

Bhutan, Kingdom of 103

Botswana 16, 155

Brazil.......................... 22, 137, 155

business-to-business transactions
.... 92

business-to-consumer contracts....
.... 85, 86, 113

Bustamante Code 128

capacity of volition and action .. 83

choice of forum.................... 72, 117

choice of governing law 8, 9, 94
categories of material law 19

choice of law.............12, 34, 36, 55,
65, 71, 92, 93, 102, 110, 139

civil law 50, 83

classification of the rules of law
character of ruling.................. 18
end of ruling 18
essence of ruling..................... 18
main idea................................ 18
nature of ruling....................... 18
sphere of application 17

conflict of law
principles....29, 51, 55, 61, 74, 78,
80, 89, 93, 102, 107, 112

regulation......13, 42, 47, 60, 64,
71, 74, 77, 80, 83, 85, 88, 94,
98, 104, 115, 122

rule............................... 14, 28, 141
character............................... 20
cross-border   corporate
relations........................... 39
delimitation of legitimate
regulatory interests......... 26
intermediary role of 25
international   organizations,
formulated by 39
legal categories of 14, 77, 92,
100
private international law
disputes........................... 39
structure............................... 20
system of material law rules
.... 24
unity of aim and means 26
territorial settlement of 51

conflicting regulatory interests ... 6,
12, 18, 21, 24, 39, 103, 125, 129

Convention   on   Private
International Law 128

corporate freedom............... 34, 137

corporate law
objective 71

corporate law rule 24

corporate nationality.....................
.... 47, 48, 59, 88, 89, 92, 120

corporate obligations 77

corporate property 48

corporation................................. 57
appropriate law form............ 109
as independent subjects of law
.... 47

as subject of a private international law dispute....42

choice of management scheme 109

choice of the currency 109

choice of the place where to establish / re-establish 109

choice of the state in which to open banking accounts 109

corporate contract......90, 98, 102

corporate personality 138

corporate property. ....
48, 55, 73, 76, 100, 102, 115, 117, 129, 136

definition.................................46

formation of.............................89

free will 109

governance and control 73

guarantees 140

insolvency and termination ...90

legal personality......................73

legal status of...............78, 87, 92, 114, 123, 125, 129, 143

limited liability of incorporators 73

multiple nationality...........48, 94

national law of 89

origins of.................................45

reorganization of 90

representation of......................90

responsibility..........................140

right to change or terminate a corporate activity...............109

shareholders participation 90

social accountability..............140

solidarity................................140

cross-border corporate disputes international jurisdiction over 114

cross-border corporate relations 17, 41, 43, 62, 70, 71, 78, 87, 93, 95, 104, 139, 141, 147

jurisdictional problems 1

public policy 2

system of law and jurisdiction 1

cross-border labour relations 96

Czech Republic.................. 100, 156

delimitation of interests of different states 41

Denmark 117

deregulation............................. 137

directly applicable rules................
5, 7, 18, 26, 29, 35, 39, 51, 53, 78, 86, 91, 107, 116, 143

domicile.................................. 53, 81

economic capability 139

England 13, 22, 39, 83, 115, 128

Common Law 13

EU Laws 13

EU Member States 92

European Convention On Human Rights...................................... 13

European Economic Area 88

external liberty of law enforcers 25

family rights 79, 83

foreign court judgments, enforcement of....................... 49

foreign decisions recognition of......................... 122

foreign element definition................................. 52

foreign judgements prior conditions for.............. 121

foreign legislator will of..................................... 65

forum rei sitae 100

forum shopping......................... 109

France ....
3, 4, 11, 14, 20, 28, 48, 58, 59, 79, 80, 83, 86, 98, 100, 114, 156
French Civil Code 11, 156

freedom of contract.......................
.... 84, 86, 125, 143

freedom of establishment........... 63

fundamental individual rights .. 82

general acts 40, 116

Germany................................ 14, 89

Ghana.. 106

good faith conduct 80

governing law............................ 132

Greece 117

Hungary 129

idea of private law 52

individual freedom ....
.... 34, 57, 107, 113, 136, 141

international agreements
recognition of........................... 12

international law rules 24, 120

international legal acts
conflict of law rules................. 39
material law regulation of private international law.... 39

internationality, element of . 24, 42

interstate trade and commerce 135

inviolability of a contract 111

inviolability of law 11, 58, 61

Iraq........................ 98, 105, 121, 155

Israel
Proclamation of Independence
.... 31

Italy 4, 14, 72, 116, 119

jurisdiction
appropriate...................................
.... 6, 36, 43, 49, 59, 111, 145
choice of 64, 102
conflicting 49
foreign 11
international5, 12, 26, 39, 51, 53, 107, 110, 111, 114, 117, 119, 122, 135, 141, 142, 143
national courts 117
of courts 72
problems.....2, 6, 36, 53, 60, 109, 111, 114, 126, 130, 132, 141
prorogation of 110, 119
scope of 115

jurisprudence
governing law 6
procedural law.......................... 6
public interest 6

Justinian 21, 79, 153

labour
rights 98
sanctity of 137

law of continuity........................ 59

legal institute
test of 126

legal paternalism 77, 84

legal personality 46, 57, 70, 73

legal rights and obligations...........
.... 17, 36, 43, 133, 146

legal status of individuals 43, 83

legitimate regulatory interests.......
.... 36, 51, 134, 142, 145

lex causae 22, 37, 105, 113

lex fori 12, 13

lex loci 76, 100
use of 95

lex loci actus..................... 77, 78, 107

lex loci celebrationis 107

lex loci contractus.........103, 107, 112

lex loci delicti..................77, 104, 107

lex loci delicti commissi..........77, 107

lex loci laboris...............................106

lex mercatoria 51, 126, 127, 146

lex originis.....................................89

lex personalis...
...55, 76, 83, 87, 99, 100, 107, 113
   use of 79, 86

lex rei sitae.....................55, 100, 107

lex societatis ....
   42, 55, 62, 75, 78, 80, 84, 89, 91,
   95, 98, 107, 113, 128, 129, 142
   use of 87

lex specialis derogat generali 40

lex voluntatis......77, 80, 84, 113, 128
   use of 107

limited liability...........................136

Luxemburg 117

Magna Carta...............................128

Malawi 11
   Constitution of the Republic of
   ....10, 155

material law principles ....
   ....10, 47, 52, 55, 77

material law rules................28, 141

mechanism of ruling 16

merchants 127

Monaco
   Constitution..............................9

multinational corporations.........55

nationality of a corporation........63

natural justice...............................14

natural law 69, 80

Netherlands 117

non-extinguishment of rights....37

Ottoman Empire 98

party autonomy.........................109

permanent residence 53, 81, 82

philosophy of law 43, 45, 132

place of incorporation 70

place of incorporation or
   registration..............................63

Poland................... 4, 59, 62, 64, 156

positive law....................................
   ....54, 69, 70, 82, 111, 125, 131
   objective....................................70

practical law
   main purpose of 38

private international law 49
   definition.....................................3
   distinct legal systems................4
   foreign property 43
   history of 5, 12
   nature and essence of 3
   of obligations 43
   of physical persons 33, 43
   rights and duties 37
   rules ....
   ..7, 40, 71, 78, 97, 125, 131, 141

private international law of
   corporation
   attributes of..............................33
   choice of court system 109
   choice of legal system...........109
   current state of........................131
   definition..................................42
   definitions 1
   formal attributes of 39
   main purpose of 38
   method of regulation..............78
   objective..............................70, 71

principles in 53
prospects and problems of... 135
purpose...................................... 78
questionable points........... 60, 64
scale of 125
scope of............................ 69, 114
subject matter of regulation... 78
terminology.............................. 44
private international law relations
.... 49
private law
rights and obligations............. 31
private law instrument, choice of
.... 77
private law relations
equity 85
subject of.................................. 85
private law rights and obligations
5, 19, 25, 40, 44, 51, 66, 73, 80,
83, 85, 93, 115, 117, 145
private property
sanctity of 136
procedural law 132
proper and improper law,
boundary between 12, 13
proper law......................................
.... 21, 43, 49, 96, 105, 114, 145
property
rights to........................... 100, 101
sanctity of 12, 111
status of 100, 107
property, allocation of 99
prorogation agreement............. 119
public interest..................... 20, 132
public interests of states............. 99
ratio legis 125

reciprocal delimitation of powers
.... 12
reincorporation........................... 59
renvoi 7, 64, 66
retortions 23, 28, 54, 82
rights of nationality..................... 88
role of law enforcers................... 21
Roman Empire.......................... 137
Roman law 71
rule of law................................... 14
broad conception 30
legal categories of 14
narrow conception................... 27
normative 27
rules for courts........................... 78
Russia............. 3, 10, 14, 19, 99, 155
Civil Code of the Russian
Federation.............. 10, 99, 155
Serbia................................ 116, 156
sovereign rights of states.......... 141
sovereign states
informal duties of 23
sovereignty
pillars of.................................. 139
Spain...................... 20, 40, 110, 156
Spanish Civil Code.......... 20, 156
special acts.................................. 40
state of incorporation............ 63, 90
state sovereignty................... 21, 27
structural element of
private international law
relations 76
subject of law 54, 85
subject of power......................... 54
supremacy of law 79

sustainable development................
.................................8, 38, 70, 139

Switzerland 62, 91, 118

Syria...15, 58

systematization of law 8, 17

territorial operation of law ...14, 52

theory of certitude...............71, 136

theory of will...............................71

Tunisia...........................49, 117, 156

Turkey 29, 51, 66, 84, 156
    foreign law application...........29

UK ....ii, 89, 96, 104, 120
    legislation................................28

Ukraine................................. 50, 156

United States.... 58, 72, 89, 149, 155

unjust enrichment105, 106, 122, 123

USSR 4

Vietnam 129

voluntary association 136

Westphalian model.................... 35